Optimizing Back-Office Operations

Best Practices to Maximize Profitability

ZAHID KHALID

WILEY

John Wiley & Sons, Inc.

Published by John Wiley & Sons, Inc., Hoboken, New Jersey.

Published simultaneously in Canada.

For general information on our other products and services or for technical support, please contact our Customer Care Department within the United States at (800) 762-2974, outside the United States at (317) 572-3993 or fax (317) 572-4002.

Wiley also publishes its books in a variety of electronic formats. Some content that appears in print may not be available in electronic books. For more information about Wiley products, visit our web site at www.wiley.com.

Library of Congress Cataloging-in-Publication Data

Khalid, Zahid.
   Optimizing back office operations : best practices to maximize profitability / Zahid Khalid.
         p. cm.
   Includes bibliographical references and index.
   ISBN 978-0-470-53189-1 (cloth)
  1. Industrial management.   2. Profit.   I. Title.
   HD30.5.K47 2010
   658–dc22

                                                              2009041459

Printed in the United States of America

10 9 8 7 6 5 4 3 2 1

To my father, M.R. Khalid, who taught me
to live without fear.
To my mother, Alia Khalid, who taught me
to love without conditions.

Thank you for everything.
You are always with me but I still miss you!

Contents

Preface   ix

CHAPTER 1   Profits: The Reason a Business Exists   1

Profitability Defined   2
Profitability Equation and Related
  Metrics   9
Liquidity, Growth, and Financial
  Flexibility   19
Conclusion   25

CHAPTER 2   Cost and Capability: Strategic Choices   27

Capability: One Size Does Not Fit All   28
Cost: You Get What You Pay For   34
Measuring Capability   41
Conclusion   44

CHAPTER 3   Financial Supply Chain: Entering the
Gold Mine   45

What Is the Financial Supply Chain?   45
Working Capital Defined   50
Working Capital Processes   59
Conclusion   65

CHAPTER 4 Platform for Execution: A System for
Maximizing Profits   69

Process Benchmarking   74
Process Optimization   86
Process Automation   86
Process Integration   88
Process Standardization   89
Conclusion   92

CHAPTER 5 Optimizing Accounts Payable   95

Implications of A/P Effectiveness   97
Best Practices   99
Enabling Technologies   115
Conclusion   122

CHAPTER 6 Optimizing Accounts Receivable   125

Implications of A/R Effectiveness   126
Best Practices   130
Enabling Technologies   137
Conclusion   144

CHAPTER 7 Optimizing Purchasing   147

Implications of Purchasing Effectiveness   149
Best Practices   152
Enabling Technologies   160
Conclusion   168

CHAPTER 8 Optimizing Treasury Operations   171

Implications of Treasury Effectiveness   175
Best Practices   179

Enabling Technologies 193
Conclusion 200

Epilogue 203
Index 207

Preface

A ccording to Killen Associates, "A typical $1 billion company spends approximately $27 million annually on unnecessary working capital and inefficient processing functions because they lack visibility into the Financial Supply Chain."

Historically, most companies have consistently focused on the revenue-generating activities and invested heavily in organizational capabilities that support this effort. Over the last two decades, significant improvements have also been made in driving down costs and cycle times in the *physical* supply chain. Major enterprise resource planning vendors have coined acronyms such as SCM and CRM and generated healthy revenues for their companies. The corporations that bought and deployed these technology-enabled platforms have had varying results, though. Along with the success stories, there are plenty of horror stories still fresh in the minds of those who traveled along these roads to the promised land of profitability.

One of the key reasons for failing to meet the profitability expectations of these companies lies in the back office. Predominantly, these companies ignored the optimization of the *financial* supply chain (FSC) in a strategic manner. Although this very critical part of a business has seen the introduction of some point solutions from technology vendors, for the most part, the processes in this area still remain very paper-laden and manual. Being considered a cost center, the FSC processes, unfortunately, typically do not get the same consideration during the capital budgeting process as do the revenue-facing processes. This results in a business enterprise in which the front office and the back office are misaligned. The effects of this misalignment are seen in the lack of coordination between the revenue-producing components of the business and the back office. As a consequence, there is friction between employees, customers, and trading partners because the organization is failing to meet the needs and serve the interests of all stakeholders. The resulting lost opportunity to maximize profitability and enterprise value is significant. *The fundamental problem is that an organization that does not invest in optimizing its financial back office through process improvement, automation, integration, and standardization has an unbalanced cost and capability structure.* For such an organization, the knee-jerk reaction to control costs when faced with an adverse business environment is to reduce headcount, particularly in the support functions in the back office.

The idea for this book originated as a result of conversations with several senior executives and colleagues who hold leadership roles in various functions that affect working capital. A theme that emerged during these discussions revolved around cost reduction and its impact on the capabilities of the organization. None of these leaders saw cost reduction as anything but a necessary evil. The reason for that, although not often articulated, is that cost reduction has become synonymous with *headcount* reduction, reduction in product and service offerings, or lower quality standards. However, one critical element that is neglected in the reduction-focused approach to controlling costs is organizational *capabilities*. Ideally, a business would have all the capabilities it needs to be competitive and profitable at zero cost. However, that is not possible, so the obvious question that arises is one of a balance between cost and capability. This balance has a name: *optimization*; specifically, working capital optimization. This book presents a *cost-capability optimization* approach to maximizing profitability.

The specific areas that are part of the FSC include:

- Accounts payable
- Accounts receivable
- Purchasing
- Treasury—for managing the overall FSC from a performance viewpoint

The processes in these functions have a direct impact on working capital and are therefore critical to the liquidity, solvency, and profitability of a business. The metrics that are relevant to these processes are the focus of attention of the treasury and key to an efficient and value-creating treasury organization.

The book uses examples and case studies to show that cost optimization and not cost reduction is the right approach to maximizing profitability and enterprise value. Indeed, it is the only way to achieve *sustainable profitability*. In this book, the science of process improvement, the art of finance, and the enabling powers of information technology come together to make the case for a dependable approach to maximizing profitability and cash flow. The objective of the book is to make a strong case for FSC optimization as a viable strategy for profit maximization.

FSC optimization is getting a lot of attention in the finance world. This trend became mainstream in large organizations roughly around 2004. However, the current economic crisis has pushed FSC to the forefront for most organizations. Some evidence of this trend can be seen by the focus and attention given to this subject by management consulting firms, research and advisory firms, technology solutions vendors, and trade publications.

CHAPTER 1

Profits: The Reason a Business Exists

The essence of a successful business is really quite simple. It is your ability to offer a product or service that people will pay for at a price sufficiently above your costs, ideally three or four or five times your cost, thereby giving you a profit that enables you to buy and to offer more products and services.

—Brian Tracy, Chairman, Brian Tracy International

All too often, we hear and read in the business media business leaders proclaim: "Our focus is on increasing shareholder value." What is this value, and from whose perspective are they attempting to increase it? Using the definitions provided by titans of the business and investing world including Warren Buffett, Benjamin Graham, George Soros, and Peter Lynch, a shareholder with a short-term interest is merely a prospector. It is the long-term focused shareholder that is a true investor. These people are "owners of the business" in the true sense and those whose interests business leaders should be serving. Wall Street does not usually cater to their interests, and, all too often, business leaders cater more to Wall Street than to business owners. The evidence of this discrepancy between words and action surrounds us in the form of failed corporations, issues around excessive executive compensations, and accounting scandals of historic proportions.

Clearly there is a gap between what is being said and what actually is being done in this context. This gap can be translated most often into a differential of focus between short-term profit maximization and long-term sustainable profitability—on the surface it appears to be a case of harvesting low-hanging fruit. The actual causes of this phenomenon are complex and involve elements of human psychology, emotion, greed, and competitive nature. Here we look at only those aspects that are most relevant to the art and science of managing a business enterprise.

The core problem in this regard may well be linked to the historical concept of a public corporation and what exists in today's environment. The dilution of ownership and the resulting imbalance of power in favor of management are evident in the daily headline news. Government intervention in this arena in the form of limits on executive compensation and other related measures will not solve the problem. Perhaps it is time to reconsider the fundamental structure of what we call a public company.

Profitability Defined

What is profitability? Most commonly, it is understood to mean "profits." But that is not accurate. *Profit-ability* is the *ability* of a business to generate profits and it is an *ongoing state of being, a steady state* whereas profits are discrete *events in time.* In the context of long term versus short term, profits are the focus of short-term focused management whereas profitability is the focus of the longer-term focused management. We will see during the course of this book that only management that is focused on profitability is truly attempting to serve the best interests of the shareholders: the business owners.

Profits can be generated through superior operating performance as well as by using destructive short-term tactics such as unjustified plant closing, capability-destroying headcount reduction, and nonstrategic reductions in investment in new product lines and services. One name that comes to mind in this context is that of Albert John Dunlap, popularly known as "Chainsaw Al." Named by Conde Nast Portfolio magazine one of the "Worst American CEOs of All Time," he is barred by the SEC from serving as an officer or director of any public company as a result of his conduct at Sunbeam Corp. His formula for "increased profits and earnings" was to fire thousands of employees at once and close plants and factories. Wall Street loved him because of *his ability* to deliver higher earnings in a very short time. Investors (really prospectors) loved him for delivering high stock prices in a short time frame. Boards of directors loved him for his *performance.* None of these constituents bothered to ask the question that needed to be asked: What was the impact of Chainsaw Al's short-term profits-focused tactics on the *profit-ability* of the companies he was leading? Some very smart people lost sight of the difference between *profits and profitability.* During the course of his career and using his short-term profit-seeking management techniques, Chainsaw Al brought strong corporations, including Scott Paper and Crown Zellerbach, down on their knees. Dunlap was finally stopped when he attempted to use his methods to increase the share price of the Sunbeam-Oster Corporation. His plan failed when Sunbeam stock plummeted within four months after a dramatic temporary rise in price. It was discovered that Sunbeam's revenues had been padded because Dunlap had given large discounts to retailers that bought far more merchandise than they could handle. While this positively affected the income statement (albeit through some accounting creativity), the excess merchandise had to be shipped to warehouses to be delivered later and added to the inventory balance sheet account. Rising inventory made the investors suspicious, and they eventually panicked, bringing down the stock price of Sunbeam. Dunlap was fired and agreed to pay $15 million to settle a shareholder lawsuit.

Profitability is a function of the internal and external factors that have long-term implications. It is a matter of how a business enterprise structures itself internally as well as how it positions itself to face the external forces in the marketplace in which it competes. Both have a strong bearing on the long-term competitiveness of the business. The most important consideration in this regard is agility, a concept we explore later. Agility in this context is the fundamental ability of a business to respond quickly and cost effectively to external forces and to be able to execute internal strategies in the face of a constantly changing competitive environment. It is a key component of a profitable business enterprise and is actualized through its platform for execution. Agility in this sense is both operational as well as financial. The focus of this book is on financial agility.

The key external factors of financial agility include:

- Competitive landscape
- Regulatory landscape
- Industry fundamentals
- Economic conditions

These external factors are not in the direct control of the management or the business enterprise. The competitive landscape is a complex web of forces that act on the business entity and give it either a competitive advantage or a disadvantage, depending on how it has positioned itself facing externally as

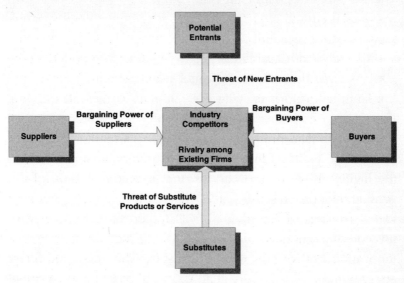

FIGURE 1.1 Porter Five-Forces Model

well as how it has organized itself internally. Michael Porter summarized this in his "Five Forces Model," as shown in Figure 1.1.[1]

Ample material has been written on defining this external environment and the various generic strategies that deal with these forces. What has been lacking is a blueprint for the execution of these strategies. As Larry Bossidy, retired chief executive of Honeywell, captured so well in his book *Execution: The Discipline of Getting Things Done*: "When companies fail to deliver on their promises, the most frequent explanation is that the CEO's strategy was wrong. But the strategy by itself is not often the cause. Strategies most often fail because they aren't executed well."[2]

The flawless execution Bossidy refers to is the domain of the internal factors of a business enterprise, which include:

- Organizational structure
- Organizational culture

- Capital structure
- Operating structure
- Management capabilities
- Upstream/downstream channel relationships
- The platform for execution

How a business chooses to carve out its market share is at the core an exercise in formulating its competitive strategy. At the highest level, it may choose one or a combination of the generic strategies—cost leadership, differentiation, segment focus. The rest of the internal factors then have to align with this core strategy decision. For example, companies that choose innovation as their core strategy must carefully plan and foster an *organizational culture* that supports innovation. A good example of this is Microsoft Corporation, where software developers are allowed a great deal of latitude in the work environment, including a very informal dress code, relaxed work environment, and casual interaction style with peers and even senior management. EDS, in contrast, has followed a *segment focus* strategy whereby it seeks customers and clients in large corporations that have traditionally valued a strict dress code and formal interaction style. Both are correct in fostering their respective cultures as each is aligned with the core strategy being executed.

Michael Porter gave this internal structure a name—the Value Chain—and suggests a generic representation as shown in Figure 1.2.

In essence, profitability speaks to the fundamental ability of the business to generate profits over the long term. Although sometimes profits may remain elusive due to external factors, the entity's ability to generate profits remains intact at its core and will give it a competitive advantage over the long term. Among the internal factors listed earlier, all are rather well understood except the last one: platform for execution. We

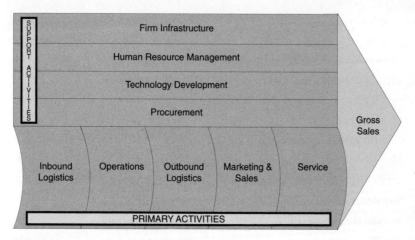

FIGURE 1.2 The Value Chain

Source: Michael E. Porter, *Competitive Advantage: Creating and Sustaining Superior Performance* (New York: Free Press, 1985).

look at this in detail in Chapter 4, but for now, it is sufficient to understand that it is the digitized embodiment of the core business processes. It is what ensures that the strategies and resources of the business are leveraged optimally to maximize profits. Meddling with the profitability capabilities of a company during an economic downturn with the intention of cost cutting is an all-too-common mistake, and a tragic one. Leading organizations have learned to develop and invest in a platform for execution that does not need to be subjected to radical cost reductions for short-term reasons.

It is the primary responsibility of senior management to focus on the internal factors that determine business profitability instead of on the quarterly results that drive the short-term stock price performance. Investor relations can be a matter of taking or conceding control. If control is conceded to short-term "prospectors" to prop up earnings, those very prospectors will take their profits and leave, since everything that is knowable about the stock is already factored into its stock price.

This may help the short-term incentive compensation goals and profits objectives of some groups, but it does not necessarily turn out to be the right thing for the longer-term prospects of the organization. Lacking this long-term focus, intentionally or otherwise, leads to the eventual decline and even demise of the business. Examples of this are all around us: Think of Countrywide, Sunbeam, and Polaroid. All of them earned healthy profits for a long time due to superior profitability but neglected to stay focused on *profitability* and either filed for bankruptcy or ceased to exist altogether.

At the most basic level, we define profits as:

$$\text{Profits} = \text{Revenue} - \text{Direct Costs} - \text{Indirect Costs}$$

The area of controlling and minimizing direct costs is mature and attended to adequately by a majority of the business organizations through the use of supply chain management and procurement practices. It is the indirect costs—which constitute a significant portion of the overall costs—that are not as well managed. This is not to say that the importance of managing indirect costs is not well understood. Rather, the manner in which costs containment is undertaken by a vast majority of the business enterprises is not aligned with the best interests of shareholders—enterprise value creation. The management techniques most often employed in this regard are reactive in nature and do not contribute to long-term profitability. When I have asked audiences in seminars and presentations to share what comes to mind when they hear the phrase "cost reduction," the answer always is "headcount reduction." Yet it does not have to be this way, nor should it be. The up-and-down, yo-yo effect of hiring and firing is destructive to the very precious resources of human capital so often spoken passionately about by senior managements across the country. There has to be a better way, and there is. This is the realm of *profitability* and *platform for execution* that is the focus of this book.

In later chapters, we examine this area more closely and see some best practices that help maximize profitability by streamlining and leveraging back-office capabilities to minimize this yo-yo effect. Some layoffs may be unavoidable; but many others are due to a lack of process optimization, automation, integration, and standardization that cause this value-destroying phenomenon.

Profitability Equation and Related Metrics

Profitability of a business enterprise is analyzed and measured in various ways, depending on the objectives of the analysis. Some of the most common measures are:

- Return on sales (ROS)
- Return on equity (ROE)
- Return on assets (ROA)
- Return on invested capital (ROIC)

The basic economic viability of the industry in which a business competes is determined by its gross margin, defined as:

(Net Revenue – Cost of Goods Sold)/Net Revenue

Although this metric varies somewhat from one firm to another within the same industry, its limits are defined by the industry as a whole. As an example, Dr Pepper Snapple Group and Pepsi Co. compete in the beverages industry segment with an order-of-magnitude difference in revenue size, with Pepsi having the larger share. In spite of the advantage enjoyed by Pepsi due to economies of scale, the cost of goods sold (COGS) metric for both organizations is very close, as depicted in Figure 1.3.

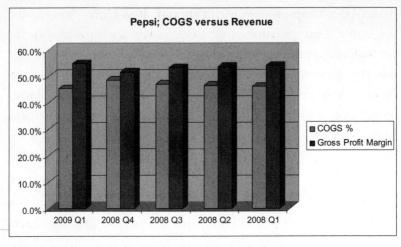

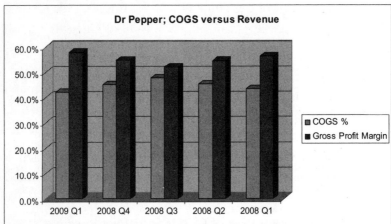

FIGURE 1.3 Cost of Goods Sold and Gross Margin

Excellence in this particular area is determined by internal capability in the procurement function. This function lies at the heart of physical supply chain management, which has a parallel on the finance side: financial supply chain, a topic we explore in detail in Chapter 3. The near equality of the ratio of COGS to revenue between the smaller Dr Pepper and the larger Pepsi indicates carefully designed and managed supply chains that close the advantage gap between the two companies in this area of margins. Although Pepsi may have more leverage with its upstream and downstream channel partners, Dr Pepper has arranged its physical supply chain to close this gap. In a similar manner, Pepsi may have advantages on the financial supply chain side, including access to capital on better terms and banking relationships that are favorable compared to its competitors. How Dr Pepper has designed, invested in, and manages it financial supply chain compared to Pepsi will determine which one of these two competitors has greater profitability—the ultimate measure of success for a business enterprise. This advantage is gained and sustained or lost in the financial back office as embodied in the platform for execution. A comparison of the efficiency of the financial back-office of these two competitors can be made by looking at their cash conversion cycle and its components, shown in Figure 1.4.

From looking at the components of the Cash Conversion Cycle, Pepsi seems to have its financial back-office in a much more stable state as well as the mix of the component metrics is what one would want to have, reflected in a DPO larger than DSO. This is not the case for DrPepper, which has declining DPO and a rising DSO, indicating a lack of efficiency and structural alignment within the financial back-office processes that affect its working capital. It should be noted, however, that the dramatic change in 2008 can be attributed to DrPepper being spun off from Cadbury-Schweppes as an independent entity.

Return on Sales

Return on sales, also called operating margin, is defined as:

$$\text{ROS} = \text{Operating Income}/\text{Net Revenue}$$

ROS is a measure of the efficiency of operations, and it is primarily what separates good management from the rest. Like

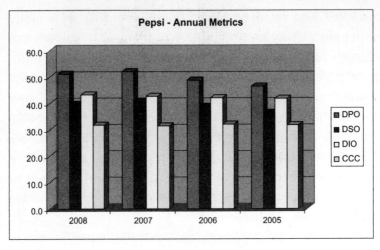

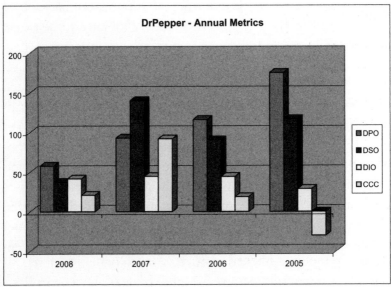

FIGURE 1.4 Cash Conversion Cycle and its Components

any other metric, though, the important factor is the long-term trend this metric follows, not just one measurement at a certain point in time. The best way to make use of ROS and the other metrics mentioned here is to compare them across competitors and with industry averages over a period of time. The key thing about ROS is that it shows the effectiveness of what is being done within the organization for internal-facing purposes that drive the competitive advantage of the business enterprise. Management has perhaps the most control over this key metric than any other. Although this metric has an influence on other metrics that are of more interest to the short-term–focused Wall Street, management cannot easily hide its manipulation. As we saw in the example of Chainsaw Al, some of the destructive tactics employed to improve this metric can be discovered in the public press. There remain, however, other accounting shenanigans that are harder to uncover.

Return on Equity

Return on equity is defined as:

$$ROE = Net\ Income/Shareholder\ Equity$$

Like all of these ratios, ROE alone is not a determinant of better value of the business. It is meant to indicate the level of return investors are receiving from their investment in the business enterprise as compared to other options they may have for investing their capital. One way to enhance this return is to use more debt in the financial structure. A business that uses greater debt is said to use financial leverage and will have a higher ROE than one with relatively smaller debt levels. However, the debt-intensive business has a higher financial risk and lower financial flexibility. The lower flexibility comes from the fact that interest payment on debt is a short-term liability and therefore affects the liquidity measures—a core concern of the treasury function as part of working capital management. The high-level check on this risk level is conducted by using the *interest coverage ratio*. Different industries, however, have different fundamental requirements for capital and of debt. ROE is best used to compare the performance of companies within

13

the same industry and also for period-over-period performance for the same enterprise.

Return on Assets

Return on assets is defined as:

$$ROA = Net\ Income/Total\ Assets$$

This is a key ratio that indicates how efficiently management is using the assets to generate profits. Again, a business with a smaller investment in assets will have a higher ROA, and that alone can be misleading in comparing businesses across industries. One key way in which this ratio is manipulated by management for short-term profits is by reducing investment in property, plant, and equipment (PP&E). This reduction in capital assets reduces the denominator in the ROA equation, resulting in a higher measure. Of course, this is not a sustainable state as these physical assets have a finite life and eventually have to be replaced. Again, the short-term focus on profits undermines the enterprise value interests of the shareholders. Let us be clear on one thing, though: There is nothing illegal about management choosing to reduce investment in PP&E. It may even be warranted by certain timing considerations to maximize the opportunity for a cost advantage to the business enterprise. However, we should be concerned when management intentionally and specifically uses tricks to enhance the ROA measure by sacrificing the long-term value of the enterprise. Enron, for example, used a technique whereby certain officers of the company owned separate business entities in which Enron had ownership interest. These entities were used to generate revenue for Enron and owned assets that were not on Enron's balance sheet. Because their profits were included in Enron's income statement to the extent of its ownership interest but the assets were not counted on Enron's balance sheet, Enron's ROA was greatly but misleadingly enhanced.

Return on Invested Capital

Return on invested capital is defined as:

$$\text{ROIC} = \text{Profit after Tax/Invested Capital H}$$

where

$$\text{Invested Capital} = \text{Total Assets} - \text{Current Liabilities}$$

ROIC is perhaps the strongest indicator of a business's financial performance as it relates to increasing shareholder value due to its ability to drive stock market multiples of book value. This metric is best used when considered along with economic profit (EP) and revenue growth (if EP is positive). EP is calculated as:

$$\text{EP\%} = \text{ROIC} - \text{WACC}$$

where

$$\text{WACC} = \text{weighted average cost of capital}$$

EP shows the percentage by which the ROIC exceeds the return that could have been earned by investing in Treasury bill plus some equity risk. This is tied to the concept of economic value added (EVA) in corporate finance. EVA is an estimate of true economic profit after making corrective adjustments to generally accepted accounting principle accounting, including deducting the opportunity cost of equity capital. Opportunity cost of equity capital is deducted because in order to correctly evaluate the financial benefit of one investment versus another—in this case investing capital back into the business enterprise or investing it in alternate comparable ventures—the cost of forgoing one or the other must be considered.

All of these measures provide insights into one aspect of profitability or another. However, none of these measures alone gives a complete picture of profitability. Each one alone does not tell us "why" the profitability, high or low, is as it is. DuPont Chemical Company created the DuPont equation to solve this problem. Developed for internal use, this formula has become widely used across all industry segments. The formula is:

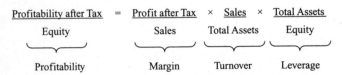

$$\underbrace{\frac{\text{Profitability after Tax}}{\text{Equity}}}_{\text{Profitability}} = \underbrace{\frac{\text{Profit after Tax}}{\text{Sales}}}_{\text{Margin}} \times \underbrace{\frac{\text{Sales}}{\text{Total Assets}}}_{\text{Turnover}} \times \underbrace{\frac{\text{Total Assets}}{\text{Equity}}}_{\text{Leverage}}$$

The formula breaks out the components that drive profitability:

- Net profit margin (NPM)
- Assets turnover
- Financial leverage

The reason it is so important to look at profitability in terms of its component parts is that firms in different industry segments have quite different profitability drivers. Even firms within the same industry have different explanations for their profitability ratios. To be effective, management must understand what is driving the profitability of the business.

High-turnover industries, such as retail and grocery stores, typically have very low profit margins but employ high asset turnover, making their cash conversion cycle (CCC) very short. The ROE of such firms may be particularly dependent on performance of the asset turnover metric, and hence it must be studied carefully to determine performance. For example, most retailers consider same-store sales as a key performance indicator (KPI). It shows the level of profits the firm is deriving from existing stores rather than showing improved profits by continually opening new stores.

Other industries, such as heavy machinery manufacturing, may derive their profitability from selling at a higher margin rather than higher sales. The DuPont equation enables analysis to determine which of the elements is dominant in any change of ROE.

Some other sectors, such as financial services, use high leverage to generate acceptable ROE. These businesses generate handsome returns for their equity owners, as was the case with the private equity funds of the late 2000s. These firms, such as the Blackstone Group, became the darlings of Wall Street for this very reason. However, their returns were severely affected as the economic conditions became more challenging and their source of capital dried up. Their high leverage imposed a greater interest expense burden, and earnings suffered. This story is well documented in their stock prices over the past few years.

The ROA ratio developed by DuPont helps evaluate how effectively assets are used. It measures the combined effects of profit margins and asset turnover.

In order to understand the individual ratios and their impact on profitability, one can follow a logic tree as shown in Figure 1.5.

In this diagram, if the profits are being driven by the profit margin, we can look further into its subcomponents to determine where this margin is coming from. How the gross margin compares to the industry average speaks to the efficiency and effectiveness of the procurement and supply chain management function. This tells us whether the firm is paying too much for its COGS and how effective its sourcing strategies are.

FIGURE 1.5 Profitability Equation Logic Tree

We can also look at the overhead costs, also called sales, general, and administrative (SG&A), and see how the firm compares to the industry average. Keeping in mind that these cost comparisons are being done relative to sales, difference between firms' revenue size is accounted for. The comparison is in terms of a ratio. A low SG&A that supports higher profits over the long haul is a result of well-engineered and optimized back-office support functions including human resources, tax, treasury, accounts payable, accounts receivable, procurement, and information technology, among others. In this regard, it is very important to see if this number is declining or staying constant. The reason for this is related to the common tactic of trimming overhead to prop up profits to make the numbers look favorable. This method is not sustainable for any firm. In the long term, it is the right combination of capabilities and cost that make the difference. Cutting costs to reduce capability for the sake of making the numbers look good is like throwing the baby out with the bathwater. Only a management focused on the short term would take such actions that are not aligned with the core interests of shareholders.

We can also look at asset turnover to see how much it is contributing to profits. Looking at this ratio gives us insight into the efficiency of accounts receivable management via days sales outstanding, inventory management via days inventory outstanding, and the cash conversion cycle. These insights are crucial to understanding the health of the firm and, indirectly, its working capital.

Last, we can look at the leverage component of the profits to see how much it is influencing the results. Here we want to be watchful of a strong number for times interest earned. Although this varies from industry to industry, as a general rule, a high number is desirable—the higher the better. A low number indicates financial risk as the firm is not earning enough to cover the cost of interest on its debt. This is the typical risk a highly leveraged firm takes. In some instances, the debt covenants alone may drive management to take actions that are not in the firm's best long-term interests but are forced on the firm by the debt holders who seek to minimize risk to their investment.

Ultimately, maximizing profitability boils down a very simple idea: A business uses cash to invest capital in creating products or services. It then sells these products or services at a profit and receives payment from its customers. This converts the cash invested into the business back into cash. The greater the velocity, frequency, and magnitude of this cash-to-cash conversion process, the more profitable the business. The magnitude is defined by the profit margin while the velocity and frequency is embodied in the CCC. Optimizing the back office for maximum profitability entails focusing on this CCC.

Liquidity, Growth, and Financial Flexibility

Liquidity, the lifeblood of a business, is a metric that gets ample focus and attention from senior management. The treasury function spends a significant proportion of its resources on managing liquidity. The liquidity level of a business enterprise is a direct result of the general operational characteristics of the business and its strategic decisions in terms of leverage, both operating and financial. What is usually not considered in depth, however, is the influence the core working capital processes of the enterprise have on this crucial metric of an organization's health.

Growth is the objective of every business, small and large. But growth beyond a certain point is not advisable unless certain fundamental financial policy targets are revised and adjustments are made accordingly. The name for this level of growth is sustainable growth rate (SGR).

Financial flexibility is the ability of a business to react to unforeseen events and circumstances in a manner that results in increased advantage and shareholder value. It is a direct result of:

- Debt to equity ratio (D/E)
- Liquidity

A firm with high D/E ratio and low liquidity will not have the financial flexibility to react to adverse situations effectively. However, a firm with a low D/E ratio and ample liquidity will be able to maximize its advantage in the face of unforeseen events. For example, if interest rates increase (an external environment factor), a firm with financial flexibility would be able to maintain its net profit margin by borrowing less to support its operations. It would fund its working capital needs by using the cash generated by its operations. A firm that does not have this financial flexibility will be forced to borrow at a higher interest cost to support its working capital needs, thus sacrificing its net profit margin. The key to achieving this financial flexibility lies in having a fundamental ability to generate ample cash for working capital needs while using financial leverage to generate high returns for equity investors. This in turn implies that the firm's CCC should be short and net profit margin high—both of which ultimately depend on the efficiency and effectiveness of the core business processes. Achieving this financial flexibility requires creating a platform for execution that relieves the chief financial officer (CFO) from the ongoing operational aspects of the financial back office to focus on the value creating aspect of his or her responsibilities. This balancing of the balance sheet to maintain financial flexibility is a constant focus of the office of the CFO. Although using less financial leverage with a lower D/E ratio adversely affects the ROE metric, it does provide a firm with more financial flexibility. The question becomes one of enjoying opportunistic growth through higher financial leverage at times while maintaining a low D/E ratio in the longer term. This is a long-term-focused management decision that uses more financial leverage only in the short term. The result is sustainable profitability and increased shareholder value for the long term.

The discussion on this topic would not be complete without a few words on what is called the *agency problem*—a conflict of interest arising among creditors, shareholders, and management because of differing goals. In the early days of the corporation, shareholders typically were a very small, closely knit group of people. Insofar as the business entity was concerned, their interests and goals were mostly aligned. Management in this case truly "worked" for the shareholders. The agency problem was under control since the management served at the pleasure of the shareholders. This was the case for family-owned businesses in the past and remains the same for privately held corporations of all sizes today. As times changed and the number of investors grew, the control structure of the corporation changed significantly. As a result, today things are vastly different. The number of shareholders is very large for the typical public company. Although the board of directors theoretically represents the shareholders, in practice this is not always true. The board members of most of the firms are themselves officers of other firms. This creates a climate in which doing the right thing for shareholders is not always clearly defined or easy. Shareholders still have a say, albeit it is a reactive one. When poor management decisions result in a drop in the stock price, shareholders may sell their shares, usually at a loss. This certainly is not sufficient control for shareholders, whose only remedy is limited and after the fact and results in incurring a loss.

Warren Buffett is credited as being the most successful "stock market investor" in history. However, this is not accurate. His success, through Berkshire Hathaway, is a direct result of the fact that he buys most companies either entirely or secures a controlling interest in them. The nature of his "shareholding" is quite different from the average shareholder since the company officers are his employees. Just as in the old days, there is no agency problem.

No doubt this issue is a complex one. By no means am I suggesting that all of those who are engaged in managing public companies are out to enrich themselves at the expense of shareholders. However, facts and historical evidence (Enron, WorldCom, Tyco, Global Crossing, and many others) bear out the fact that ample opportunity exists for managers of public companies to short-change shareholders. And if the purpose of a business enterprise is to maximize shareholder value, then what does the agency problem mean for the reason of existence of a business?

Japanese companies can be used as a great lesson in this regard. Toyota, for example, has remained at the top of its industry through good economic times and bad. A key to its success has been the fact that when something adverse occurs that requires cost cutting, top executives take a significant cut in pay. Given that the Japanese executives are not nearly as well compensated as their western counterparts, the cut in compensation is material. The effect is twofold: It puts the pain where it belongs, and it fosters loyalty at the lower levels of the organization during turbulent times when morale problems are a serious concern. When the loyal and motivated human resources of the company rally behind management they trust and respect, it is no wonder the firm pulls through turbulent times.

It is interesting to note that 78% of companies interviewed for a University of Washington study admitted to artificially smoothing earnings and sacrificing shareholder value in order to meet or beat Wall Street expectations. Fifty-five percent also said they would avoid initiating a project with a very positive net present value if it meant falling short of the current quarter's consensus on earnings.[3] This phenomenon should be alarming to all of us engaged in the business of managing, investing in, and working for public corporations.

When corporate scandals started to hit the headlines in the United States and more recently Europe, legislators' response was swift and efficient. Amid a flurry of reviews, consultations, and debates about business ethics, a whole new set of legislation was introduced in an attempt to restore faith in capital markets. On both sides of the Atlantic, much of this effort was focused on regulatory and corporate governance issues. This was hardly surprising, considering the nature and magnitude of the problems. In addition, it is unlikely that the focus on corporate governance and regulation is going to wane anytime soon, despite the inevitable industry backlash. The reforms continue and, for many, the effects of Sarbanes-Oxley in the United States and the new Combined Code in the United Kingdom are starting to be felt. There is a danger, however, that this attempt to improve the way in which companies are regulated and governed will detract from the basics of value creation. Good corporate governance may be a necessary prerequisite but will not by itself lead to superior performance—which is, after all, what investors want and expect in return for their money.

Case Study

A $1 billion company in the healthcare industry needed to grow its operations in order to gain deeper penetration and brand recognition in the marketplace. The board engaged a consulting firm that specialized in benchmarking and analyzing the overall performance of the firm to provide fresh insights into creating a road map for transformation. The findings from benchmarking and process analysis revealed that the inefficiency of its back-office processes in general and the financial back office in particular were creating a drag on its margins. This weakness in the margins was affecting the company's ability to expand as it wanted and could be remedied through a realignment of the processes with the corporate objectives.

The fundamental issue was the lack of strong governance and weak controls within the core processes. This situation was further worsened by the highly manual nature of the processes. As a result, the organization was going through a high turnover in personnel, which not only impacted its operations in terms of the quality of care it could provide to its patients but also morale issues for its own personnel. Management was focused on keeping the work flowing through long shifts and extensive manual checking of reports to detect problems. Usually this checking could not be done until after the fact, leading to issues in patient care that impacted the company's brand image.

Turning around the situation required an investment in its core processes. Taking a fresh approach following the recommendations of the outside firm, senior management stepped back from focusing on the next few quarterly results and devoted their energies and resources to making fundamental improvements in operational and back-office processes. The improvements combined changes in its governance structure and mechanisms, policies, and procedures and in operational and financial processes.

After an 18-month effort that engaged its personnel at all levels, the organization emerged as a superb example of a business entity that was built for "profitability," not just profits. The quality of patient care was high, personnel morale was improved significantly, employee turnover and absenteeism were the lowest it had ever been, operating costs were lower and predictable, and management was able to confidently project operational results. This change enabled the company to raise the capital it needed on favorable terms to expand into the marketplace.

Conclusion

Changing a focus from profits to profitability is a critical first step toward making an organization "Built to Last."[4] The fortunes at DuPont and General Electric were not built by management focused on the short term. These giants of the American business landscape have lasted a long time and seen the ups and downs that come with such longevity. Their operating models and supporting processes leverage a platform for execution that is geared toward fundamental profitability, not merely profits.

It may seem like a trivial matter that is obvious to many, but thinking about the long term and making decisions on that basis is not something that many companies appear to commit to. It takes courage to excel and faith in the capabilities of the organization to ride out the storms of the marketplace. Of course, this means having built the capabilities needed to weather these storms in the first place. Doing this requires investing in those core capabilities. This act of investment itself is evidence of a long-term focus. It is not the same as using cost cutting as the primary tool to improve earnings during a downturn. Rather, it is an approach that seeks to minimize the drag on revenues at all times through an optimized and stream-lined platform for execution.

Notes

1. Michael E. Porter, *Competitive Advantage: Creating and Sustaining Superior Performance* (New York: Free Press, 1985).
2. Larry Bossidy and Ram Charan, *Execution: The Discipline of Getting Things Done* (New York: Crown Business, 2002).
3. John R. Graham, Campbell R. Harvey, and Shiva Rajgopal, "The Economic Implications of Corporate Financial Reporting," January 11, 2005, www.faculty.fuqua.duke.edu/~charvey/Research/Working_Papers/W73_The_economic_implications.pdf.
4. Jim Collins and Jerry I. Porras, *Built to Last: Successful Habits of Visionary Companies* (New York: Harper Business, 2004).

CHAPTER 2

Cost and Capability: Strategic Choices

A sponge has that much absorbent capability and after a while you can pour water over it and nothing stays.

—Itzhak Perlman

No business can survive and thrive without sufficient profit-generating capabilities. Ideally, a business would be able to perform all profit-generating functions at zero cost. As that is not the case in the real world, the fundamental question that arises is this: At what cost should a business perform those functions that are absolutely necessary for generating profits? There are two components to answering this question:

1. What functions (capabilities) are necessary for generating profits?
2. How much of these capabilities are needed, and at what cost?

The two components are intimately connected and cannot be managed separately without adverse implications to the business. Each business enterprise must address both components in a way that achieves the desired balance that supports the organization's strategic objectives. Defining this desired balance lies at the heart of strategic planning. This chapter outlines an approach for defining this balance in a general sense.

Capability: One Size Does Not Fit All

In the context of profitability, when we speak of capability we mean the various functions of the business that are essential to achieving its strategic goals. These functions can be categorized as either revenue generating or supporting in nature. For the scope of this book, when we speak of capability, we mean these financial back-office functions that affect its working capital:

- Accounts payable
- Accounts receivable
- Purchasing (procurement)
- Treasury

For each of these functions, the first question that needs to be asked is whether it will play a strategic role or a tactical one. This designation will be determined by the needs of the business enterprise in terms of its capabilities, which in turn are driven by the high-level competitive strategy it has chosen to pursue. In this regard, the capabilities serve to support and strengthen the core competency of the enterprise. For example, if cost leadership is the chosen strategy, then supply chain management will have to be a core competency, and this will require strong procurement capabilities. However, if innovation is the leading strategy, then the research and development (R&D) function will need to be particularly strong, and this will require a corporate culture that attracts, retains, and rewards creative people. The organization's tolerance for mistakes in pursuit of a product that delivers market advantage, for example, will have to be higher than that of another firm that is pursuing a cost leadership strategy. In essence, a business enterprise needs a strategic capabilities matrix; this matrix must be the ultimate driver of its decisions regarding investments in projects.

When capabilities are considered in this manner, they truly act as strategic weapons for the benefit of the business enterprise. Dell Corporation, for example, uses its procurement and supply chain management capability as a strategic weapon. The market advantage Dell has gained from this capability has resulted in a negative working capital situation in which Dell collects its revenues in advance of its payments to its suppliers. Without this capability and its collection of revenues ahead of its cash outlays to its suppliers, negative working capital would not be a good sign—it would indicate a liquidity crisis for Dell. By carefully choosing its competitive strategy and then focusing on the key capabilities that support that strategy, Dell has invested in its core competencies. It performs other functions well enough, but it invests heavily in those that are keys to its success through its chosen strategy.

The second question that needs to be asked is: Can the function be performed better by a third party or the business itself? Answering this question entails consideration not only of factors such as cost and quality of process but also the culture of the business. In general, if the function is not a core competency and no incremental risk arises from outsourcing it, then it should be a candidate for outsourcing. As an example, it is a well-established practice to outsource executive searches at most medium to large corporations. With their deeper contacts and knowledge of the marketplace, outside search firms can bring better-qualified candidates to the organization. However, a single-minded focus on cost is a common mistake in this regard. When outsourcing, most companies focus too much on cost and not enough on capabilities. This is a tactical approach that is focused on the short term. It can and often does lead to adverse strategic outcomes.

Once again, Dell provides a good example of this mistake. In an effort to reduce its costs after the dot-com bust of early 2000s, Dell outsourced its customer help desk function to an offshore provider. The decision was well supported by the numbers, which indicated material cost savings. However, what was not anticipated was the nonfinancial aspects of the decision: the impact on customers. Due to linguistic and cultural differences, Dell customers were very displeased with the service quality of the offshore customer help desk provider. Due to the outcry from its customer base, Dell had to reverse its decision and bring the function back in-house[1]. To its credit, Dell responded to its customers' voice, but it was a painful lesson to learn.

Once a firm has a clear understanding of which core competencies are needed and therefore which capabilities are key to success, it can gauge the *level* of each capability required to support the strategy. For this purpose, a firm needs to consider performance factors for the functions including:

- Capacity
  - What volume of work will the function need to support in any given period of measurement?
  - What type and volume of nontransactional (analytical) bandwidth will be needed?
- Throughput
  - What is the acceptable cycle time for these transactions?
  - What amount of wait time is acceptable?
- Quality
  - What error rates are acceptable?

- Is quality control better placed upstream or downstream?
- Cost
  - What is the maximum cost per transaction (unit cost) that is acceptable?

Considering these performance factors protects decision makers from making a less than optimal decision. A firm that leaves any of these considerations out risks making a lopsided decision that may result in subpar business performance.

Capacity is a measure of the volume of the work that a business function would be able to support in a sustainable manner at a desired level of quality. It is a consideration of the best estimated steady state volume of business activity that needs to be supported—not the unplanned spikes in volume. The spikes can be handled through other means and their costs estimated accordingly. Let's take an example of an accounts payable (A/P) function in a business that is considering embarking on a strategy of growth through acquisition. One of the ways in which it could support this strategy in the A/P function is to create a shared services organization (SSO) that includes A/P. The logic behind this is one of economies of scale and specialization very much along the Adam Smith line of thinking. It would be wise also to consider automating the A/P process to the extent possible that it can support the additional workload without having to continue to add staff. What also may make sense is to carefully evaluate whether to keep the clerical components of the end-to-end process in house or outsource them. Building capacity does not have to be done by building in-house resources alone. There is a rich world of providers out there that can support the operational needs of just about any business model in a very cost-effective manner. The key lies in:

- Knowing the business competitive strategy.
- Identifying the core competencies that would enable this strategy.
- Focusing on strengthening the functional capabilities that would realize the core competencies.

The rest is a matter of skillful negotiations and contract management. The challenge is to follow an objective approach to get to the point of making the decision in a timely manner, since a lack of timely decision making destroys value.

One of the recurring themes in corporate America lately has been the mass drive to pursue a capability that is fueled by buzzwords. Granted, some of these buzzwords are supported by real business value that can be realized. It is the manner in which this perceived value is pursued that leads to trouble. A good example of this is the buzzword wave of enterprise resource planning (ERP) systems in the late 1990s and early 2000s. In a rush to get their hands on the capabilities promised by the ERP systems, many businesses neglected to carefully consider what value the capability would provide. It is not a question of the validity of the value promised by the system but a question of whether the capability is aligned with the strategic objectives of the business. Just because a capability may help produce better reports or reduce headcount should not be a justification for pursuing it. Unfortunately, some companies learned this lesson the hard way after wasting tens of millions of dollars on ERP implementations that never paid off.[2] Similar stories surround the rush to outsource and offshore support functions resulting in the crippling of many profitable businesses. Again, it is not to say that these options are without benefit. Rather, ask: What capability do we need, and what is it worth to us? Once the return on investment (ROI) objectives in this analysis are met by a combination of cost and capability, obsessively trying to lower costs further is counterproductive. The reason is that there is always an opportunity cost for delaying a benefit that can be had today. A brief case study will help to drive this point home.

A large service firm with several offices nationwide was looking to manage its indirect costs better. One of the areas of attention was A/P. The firm had an A/P staff person at each office as well as corporate A/P staff at headquarters. The financial benefit of centralizing the function and stream-lining and automating the process was determined to be an annual $1.1 million reduction in operating costs, with a payback period of less than eight months. The management team responsible for making the decision, however, got bogged down in wanting to find the best deal possible with the automation technology solution provider. Keeping in mind that enterprise systems prices are not published and that the ROI figure the decision-making team was working with indicated that the vendor's proposed cost would indeed deliver on the ROI, the team should have decided to move forward and attained a better position from a cost-capability point of view. This management team, however, continued to split hairs in trying to find the next lower price offer at an opportunity cost of $91,667 per month. It spent a year trying to find the next lower price, which did materialize since technology gets cheaper as times goes by. The company was able to lower its annual cost, but on a net present value (NPV) basis over three years, it lost value.

A good and necessary starting point for determining what capabilities are needed by a business enterprise is to determine and define the *operating model* for the business. Whereas a platform for execution is the necessary level of business process automation, integration, and standardization, the operating model comprises the core structural components of the business for delivering goods and services to the customers. For example, the operating model for Southwest Airlines contains these key structural components:

- Flight Operations
- Reservations
- Fleet Maintenance
- Customer Service

When you think about the importance of having a clearly defined operating model as key to long-term revenue generation, it makes perfect sense. After all, a business is all about creating and serving customers at a reasonable profit. This model informs and commits everyone in the business enterprise to how the company will operate. The key benefit of a well-defined operating model is that the outcomes become clearly understood and predictable and the required inputs become obvious. With this knowledge in hand, the business can go about optimizing inputs and outcomes to enhance shareholder value.

Cost: You Get What You Pay For

Zig Ziglar, the famous motivational speaker, salesman, and trainer, tells an anecdote about how you get what you pay for. His son asked for a new bicycle. Zig considered the bike to be far too expensive and told his son to settle for a cheaper bike on the basis of price. Unfortunately, by the time Zig got finished replacing handlebars, tires, and other parts on the cheaper bike, it ended up costing him far more than the one his son originally picked, both in dollars and time spent.

There is nothing wrong with a low-cost support function if it provides all the capabilities the business strategy demands. However, focusing on cost alone does not serve the longer-term objectives of the organization. Even very savvy management teams have fallen victim to the desire to trim costs beyond the point where the organizational capabilities are adversely affected. Remember the story of Dell outsourcing its customer service help desk function to an offshore provider?[3] The valuable lesson we can learn from this example is that not all costs are tangible, even though they may be equally important. The cost incurred due to an unsatisfied customer is very real and can be measured in various ways, including:

- Acquisition cost of a customer
- Opportunity cost of lost referrals and repeat sales
- Dollar cost of making the customer satisfied again
- Brand image deterioration

Costs incurred by a business enterprise often are justified quite elaborately by revenue growth projections. This was the case with dot-coms. Their revenue growth projections were truly impressive. But the question that must be asked is this: Is all revenue growth good? The answer is a resounding no. As Warren Buffett says:

> *The value of any business is determined by the cash inflows and outflows—discounted at an appropriate interest rate.*[4]

This statement is founded in the basic principle of time value of money, which states that a dollar earned a year from now is worth less than a dollar earned today. By what amount it is less depends on the discount rate used. The dot-coms grew at impressive rates but generated no after-tax profit and therefore had a *negative* economic profit. And growth with negative economic profit destroys shareholder value and ultimately is not sustainable. It is not hard to find examples of management decisions that do not take long-term value into account. In many cases, these value-destroying decisions are not driven by greed or dishonesty; rather they are the result of pursuing legitimate business objectives, such as growth or increasing market share. The problem often is that some managers lack a fundamental understanding of the difference between decisions that lead to higher profits and those that create value. The primary reason for this lack of understanding is related to the inherent weakness of traditional methods of deciding which projects a business should undertake. These traditional methods rely on NPV analysis using a hurdle rate, but few companies take a portfolio approach to select projects that may not add value individually but provide capabilities that are critical to the value-creating results of other projects. The solution to this problem lies in using a structured approach to value mapping at the enterprise, business unit, and functional level for selecting projects to invest in. Only by making a connection to value creation can a project be truly qualified or disqualified for investment purposes. Lean methodology and tools can facilitate this work efficiently.

Costs come in various forms. For a product business, the most obvious form of cost is raw materials, which is reflected in its cost of goods sold account. For a services firm, the cost takes shape primarily as the people who determine the quality and speed of processes through which the firm delivers its services. It is estimated that up to 50% of the cost of service for a service business is embedded in its service delivery processes. The cost in this case is a factor of error rates and speed of delivery. The higher the error rates and slower the process execution, the higher the cost. Following our earlier thinking of determining the key capabilities necessary for supporting the competitive strategy of a business enterprise and then investing in the functions that enable those capabilities, it would be logical to conclude that service firms invest rather heavily in their people. As we all know, that is exactly the message we hear in the media. But does it match reality? The answer lies in the fates of service firms over the long term. Certainly short-term profits and the resulting high stock valuations are there for the taking for firms that would sacrifice their most precious resource: the people, by chosing headcount reduction as the first tool to react to adverse market conditions. But the long-term advantage belongs to those business enterprises that stay true to their well-thought-out strategies and focus on flawless execution even in the face of adverse economic times.

We are all quite familiar with Wal-Mart. It is the undisputed leader in executing a cost leadership strategy. There has been ample coverage in the news media of its allegedly ill impacts on Small Town USA and its style of negotiations with vendors that borders on abuse. One would think that Wal-Mart must have invested heavily in its supply chain management and procurement functions. Yes, it has, but not to the extent one would expect. What is less well known is that Wal-Mart considers its information technology function a key enabler of its strategic advantage. The availability of actionable bidirectional information flows, such as local weather reports to support merchandising decisions at the store level, are the true force behind Wal-Mart's explosive growth and success. This information availability has allowed Wal-Mart to get to the point where its size leverage reduces its cost to the point where it simply drives the competition out of business. Regardless of the emotions of the populace, which is a subject entirely for another

37

book, Wal-Mart management has clearly taken the long-term view for quite some time and has succeeded in increasing shareholder value. It is now reaping the rewards of creating positive economic value.

Let's take another example of cost reduction. In recent years, American corporations in particular and western companies in general have been outsourcing their information technology (IT) functions on a rather large scale. This trend strongly took hold after the Y2K scare blew over and management teams across the nation realized that they had tapped into a rich mine of IT resources. We are speaking here of what transpired as a result of Y2K. In the late 1990s, companies came to the realization that their mainframe (mostly) systems were programmed to handle a two-digit year as in 1994 being coded as 94. The programmers of these systems some 30-odd years earlier never gave a second thought to what would happen when the twenty-first century began. Back then, computer memory was a very scarce and precious (expensive) resource. In order to minimize the cost of the hardware needed to run the software, the software engineers decided to use a two-digit representation of a year. Essentially this meant that since the date for any computer record was stored as a two-digit number, it was not "obviously" possible to distinguish between two dates such as 1924 and 2024, with both dates being represented in the computer record as 24. Panic spread across the developed world as this "flaw" was "discovered," and fears of mayhem were fueled by those who would profit from it at the expense of the less knowledgeable. If we pause to think about it, what could possibly happen if a computer could not tell if the date was in the twentieth or the twenty-first century? (Keep in kind that we are not talking about NASA Mission Control systems or the National Missile Defense Systems here; in those cases, we would be rightfully worried about when a rocket with a nuclear warhead may have been programmed to fly off

38

by default.) In reality, in the worst-case scenario, Social Security checks might have been delayed if the computer program logic was such that it was assumed that a person was no longer alive in 2024 if he or she was born in 1924. However, the panic that spread across the country opened the floodgates for Indian programmers to come and "fix the problem." Most of the American programmers who had written the original code had retired already, and the new generation of American programmers was focused on new technologies. There were not enough American programmers to handle the magnitude of the Y2K problem. This opportunity was not lost on the very savvy businesspeople in the then budding Indian software industry. They provided the labor force to solve the problem and then made an offer that American management found hard to refuse: how would you like to have a programmer for $30 an hour instead of $90 an hour? Who could refuse? A massive wave of offshoring ensued that still has not abated.

This all took place between 1998 and 2001—a very short time frame indeed. One thing that has to be recognized is the impact that the decision to blindly (in most cases) outsource the IT function has had on the American economy and the capabilities of the American corporations. Some companies, such as Microsoft and Oracle, consider their software developers a key asset and steadfastly protect them from this phenomenon, but the outsourcing wave has caught most other companies in a monkey-see, monkey-do mind-set where software development is outsourced with a single-minded focus on cost reduction. Certainly there are some cases where cost reduction through outsourcing would enhance the enterprise value; there are, however, a lot more cases where the impact of outsourcing is not analyzed sufficiently. Not analyzing the capability impact and focusing solely on the cost component hurts an organization in the long term, whether it is outsourcing software development or customer service or accounting.

It pays to remember that not all costs are bad. Examples abound of the ill effects of recklessly commoditizing a capability of the business enterprise. The key point to consider is the manner in which the decision is made. In a vast majority of cases, no effort is made to consider the cost-capability balance. This management style does not bode well for the future of the American business enterprise.

As of late 2008, an interesting trend has been developing in IT outsourcing. Due to global competition, which has caused the cost gap between U.S. and Indian software programmers to diminish somewhat, as well as due to the political risks of dependency on certain parts of the world, increasingly more American corporations are slowly starting to rebuild their in-house software development capability.[5] One has to stop and think about this and what it truly means. Did it serve any long-term purpose to carve out a capability to offshore only to bring it back in house later? Isn't this just another example of the yo-yo effect of hiring and firing people en masse and the monkey-see monkey-do mentality? Is this the best that the brightest minds educated in the finest and most expensive business schools in America can come up with? Surely there is a better way.

That better way is the way of rational long-term thinking and objective decision making. Although it is not the subject of this book, the damage done by the decisions to offshore certain capabilities will take decades to undo. Enrollment in IT-related fields by U.S. students has dropped to critically low levels. The primary reason for this is the fear that there will be no jobs in that field in the future. It will take time to win back student confidence. In the meantime, we will just have to ask Congress for more H1-B visas and pray that we get the brightest minds for our money. We should also pray that we have enough money to afford those bright minds as the cost of acquiring them rises and we have no domestic resources to tap into. It takes years to make a good software engineer and only a Wall Street quarter to break one.

Measuring Capability

Capacity, velocity, and quality are the dimensions on which an organization needs to measure its capability needs. Cost is on the other end of this seesaw. The process of balancing cost and capability is best executed when a top-down approach is taken. It must begin with the organization's vision and strategy to realize that vision. Beginning with this broader view, which is also long term, enables the firm to analyze the key drivers of the strategy. Taken collectively, these drivers provide the starting point for further analysis to determine what the right set of capabilities should be and at what cost should they be achieved.

The process of determining the drivers is a crucial step in successfully balancing cost and capabilities. It must follow an objective approach that is facts based and data driven. Albeit there is the need for a certain amount of imagination and creativity, this must be guided, supported, and constrained by hard data. In essence, the approach should begin with a hypothesis, which should then be either proved or disproved through the sequential application of a logic tree. At each step of the logic tree, the facts and data either support the premise or negate it. In this systematic fashion, the analysis of each strategy driver will connect it to one or more capabilities that are crucial for that driver.

One of the most reliable but often neglected means of identifying the key capabilities and prioritizing them is the use of 360 degree value-gap analysis. This approach delivers the most value when it is not clear what the drivers of the strategy are. This is the case when a hypothesis-based approach has not led to any conclusions, meaning all hypotheses have been negated and exhausted. In these circumstances, the value-gap analysis approach can help point the way to the most beneficial areas of capability. The process begins with benchmarking the core processes. This approach differs from traditional bench-marking in that in values-gap analysis, benchmark results are not used directly to determine what metric gap needs to be addressed. Instead, the dollar value of the metric gap is calculated to determine if the gap is material. For example, say the benchmark reveals that the return on assets metric is at 98 percent as compared to the industry average. That may sound quite acceptable on the surface. However, when we assign a dollar value to this gap of 2%, we may realize that there is a material disadvantage due to this gap. Realizing the value of this gap can provide the catalyst for further analysis on how to close it. This would then lead to a calculation of the cost that is acceptable for this capability.

On the matter of evaluating the cost for a given capability, it is imperative to focus on the strategic value of the capability. Oftentimes the decision is based solely on discounted cash flow and net resent value basis. These approaches miss the opportunity for initiatives that provide strategic value to other capabilities. For example, NPV depends heavily on the hurdle rate (discount rate) used in the calculation. It does not take into account the risk level of the option, which is related. To overcome these deficiencies, large firms commonly use other models, such as the decision tree analysis, to enhance the objectivity of their decisions.

Case Study

UPS has been competing against FedEx for market share for quite some time. When FedEx introduced overnight delivery supported by a package information tracking system, it gained a definite competitive advantage over UPS. FedEx enjoyed this advantage as long as UPS was trying to simply catch up with its capability. But in the 1999-2000 time frame, UPS realized that in order to compete effectively with FedEx, it would need to increase the scope of its capability in the area of package tracking information availability. The key insight was that while package tracking information was available to customers during the air transit portion of the delivery service, it was not easily available during the on the road portion. In addition, FedEx's tracking system required the customers to install FedEx's proprietary IT platform in order to access to this information.

UPS invested in its package tracking capability by taking these key steps:

- It linked its air transit and ground transit systems to provide seamless tracking of packages.
- It built an information tracking platform that did not require any special IT investment from the customer; it used the Internet for ubiquitous and cost-effective access to critical information.
- It offered this capability to its customers at a price lower than that of FedEx.

The result of this shift was an 8% year-over-year growth rate for UPS in the overnight business in the early 2000s as compared to FedEx's 3.6%. A difference in growth rates like this results in substantial incremental enterprise value and is a direct result of focusing on balancing cost and capabilities, not just cost reduction. UPS did not focus on cost reduction directly, but it achieved a cost advantage by investing in the right capabilities.

Conclusion

In the era of global competition where capital travels at the speed of the Internet, fortunes can be made and lost in time that is getting shorter each year. Companies that were giants in their industry and previously could afford to stand back and watch a new entrant explore a new market before jumping in and squashing it now have to be much more vigilant and proactive. Blockbuster let Netflix "experiment" with the Internet channel of delivering movies, deciding that its footprint of 6,000-plus stores gave it a competitive advantage that could not be overcome. It thought wrong. The Internet has enabled a capability that negated Blockbuster's tremendous advantage. This is a classic study that makes the case for the value not only of continuously monitoring the cost and capability balance of the business enterprise but also leveraging fresh ideas from the outside to help the organization avoid getting into a strategic rut. In the end, we have to accept that cost itself is not a bad thing. The reality is that cost will always be with us in the equation of ROI; we must focus on maximizing profitability-enhancing capabilities instead of just trimming costs. Focusing on cutting costs without a deep understanding of the capabilities impacted by the cuts is a loser's game.

Notes

1. www.msnbc.msn.com/id/4853511.
2. http://wps.prenhall.com/bp_laudon_mis_9/32/8212/2102272.cw/justcontent/index.html.
3. www.msnbc.msn.com/id/4853511.
4. Berkshire Hathaway Annual Report, 1992. www.berkshirehathaway.com/letters/1992.html.
5. www.facilitiesnet.com/outsourcing/article/Many-Factors-Drive-US-Firms-to-Buck-Outsourcing-Trend-Consider-Onshoring-10702.

CHAPTER 3

Financial Supply Chain: Entering the Gold Mine

It is the increasingly important responsibility [of management] to create the capital that alone can finance tomorrow's jobs. In a modern economy the main source of capital formation is business profits.

—Peter F. Drucker

Why should a business enterprise have to pay to pay its obligations? Why should it have to pay to collect what it is owed? Why should it have to pay to utilize its funds? The short answer is that it is the cost of doing business. However, how much cost in this regard is warranted? How can it be minimized? This is the turf of financial supply chain optimization, where significant profit maximization opportunities lie hidden. This chapter focuses on these questions and is the heart of this book.

What Is the Financial Supply Chain?

The movement of goods from the source location to the market for consumption has long been a part of human history.

Humans have engaged in logistics in one form or another at various levels of sophistication for millennia. The term "supply chain" is a new one, coined in recent times along with others, such as "value chain" and "channel partners." They make good fodder for the management consulting services industry.

Historically the movement of essential information has lagged behind the movement of goods. That is not to say that the caravans in the old days did not carry news and business information. The issue was and remains the fact that information has a short life span. It does not age well, not in terms of value and relevance. Humans have been trying to find ways to speed up the information flow for as long as we have lived on this planet.

Time and space pose challenges that are just now beginning to be surmounted to a point where the speed of information flow can safeguard the value of information. Attempts to overcome this hurdle of time and space have included smoke signals, drums, and messenger pigeons. This problem has been particularly acute in the realm of business information, which also tends to require more safeguarding than personal information due to its competitive nature. Of course, military information is even more sensitive. In fact, most of the advances in logistics and information management in use in our personal and business lives today originated in the military complex.

A very interesting but not well known fact is that the Knights Templar are credited with the origins of the banking system in use throughout the world today. They also invented the means of making business information safe through the use of encryption whereby only certain parties could understand the meaning of the business data. As advanced as the Knights Templar were for their time, they still did not master the time and space elements of the information flow to a sufficient degree. Information could not travel much faster than the speed of goods transfer, and the problem of information value remained. This lack of efficiency in the flow of information resulted in a generally underperforming world economy. Poor information flow was not the only cause, but it certainly did play a key role in the world economy's underperformance. Guesswork and trial and error played a large part in commerce. People took enormous risks not because they were well calculated and hedged against but because the necessary information for making sound decisions was simply not available.

For decades, primarily as a result of the threat from Japanese manufacturers, American corporations have been focused on driving down the inefficiencies in the physical supply chain. The principles of supply chain management (SCM) have become standardized enough that ERP vendors now offer "SCM modules" within their software packages. No serious player in the ERP space exists today that does not offer some level of functionality for the SCM module.

SCM encompasses all movement and storage of raw materials, work-in-process inventory, and finished goods from the point of origin to the point of consumption. Procurement is the acquisition of goods and services at the best possible total cost, in the right quality and quantity, at the right time, in the right place, and from the right source, usually through a contract. These two functions go hand in hand as they focus on providing the necessary goods and services that constitute the value that is exchanged in a business transaction. Today, it is difficult to find a business enterprise of a meaningful size engaged in the provision of goods that does not have a SCM and procurement function as part of its organizational structure.

The physical supply chain always has had its counterpart on the information side. When the Knights Templar moved gold from Europe to Africa on behalf of their clients, the business information related to the transactions in a secured fashion also went along with the gold. At its most basic level, this transfer of information related to the transfer of physical goods is what is now called the *financial supply chain (FSC)*. The FSC, however, is more than transactional information. In the age of information that we live in today, often the information itself becomes the *value* that is being transferred in a business transaction. Consider the flow of information in the investment world, where investors and financial institutions are engaging in a bidirectional flow of information. There is no parallel physical goods transfer taking place. It is the exchange of the "ethereal" value that is being exchanged. As globalization continues to take hold, it is inevitable that the FSC will increasingly become the conduit for value exchange in its own right as opposed to playing more of a support role to the physical supply chain as we still see today. When we look at the world gross domestic product, which stands at $60.5 trillion as of end of 2008,[1] we can see the enormous amount of capital that flows through the global FSC among financial institutions, buyers, suppliers, consumers, and investors. The overall structure of a generic FSC is shown in Figure 3.1.

Business enterprises that have grasped the concept of the value of the FSC have already started making progress toward reaping the benefits of sustainable profitability. Their reward for taking the initiative has been a competitive advantage due to lower costs not only for the enterprise but across the entire supply chain. They understand that in today's world, no firm successfully stands alone for long. It is a matter of forging partnerships and alliances that create a whole that is greater than the sum of its parts. In this way of thinking, there is no room for *cost shifting,* which has been the hallmark of good financial management for a long time. That mode of thinking is obsolete and in fact detrimental to the organization and its entire supply chain. It is not conducive to win-win business relationships where all parties prosper knowing that they are

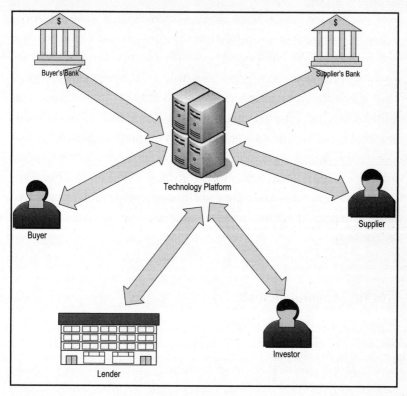

FIGURE 3.1 Generic Financial Supply Chain

not engaged in a zero-sum game. It is time for a new way of thinking where business enterprises collaborate with their strategic and channel partners to *drive costs out* of the supply chain entirely. There is no longer a need for, nor a benefit from, a tug-of-war on cost between parties that are collaborating within the physical supply chain for mutual benefit.

What is the compelling reason for taking the plunge into the world of financial supply chain? It is simple: cash. According to independent studies conducted by various research firms, *an estimated U.S. $500 billion to over U.S. $1 trillion is tied up in unnecessary working capital globally in the global FSC.* That is a significant amount of cash. If released, it could have a valuable impact on the global economy. The difficulty in this realm in the past has been the ability to capture, consolidate, analyze, and communicate actionable information in a timely and cost-effective manner. The advent of computers and particularly the Internet has removed this hurdle. The remaining challenge is one of vision, creativity, and expertise. All of these ingredients are available to any business enterprise today within its own four walls or from the outside in the form of consultants who specialize in this emerging field that combines finance, business process engineering, and information technology.

Working Capital Defined

Cash flow is the lifeblood of every business enterprise, and *working capital processes* are the arteries through which it flows. The efficiency of these processes is just as critical to the health and survival of a business organization as artery health is for a human body. Whether the firm is a start-up, a Fortune 500, or anything in between, a lack of liquidity means the business perishes. This fact is borne out repeatedly by the dot-com bust and the economic crisis that we currently face. Businesses with less than sufficient liquidity will not be able to weather this storm. Regardless of other metrics, such as growth rates, profitability, and brand recognition, this rule of finance always has and will continue to hold true.

Essentially, working capital is the amount of liquidity required by a business enterprise to continue its day-to-day operations while meeting its short-term obligations to its creditors, suppliers, and other entities, such as tax and regulatory authorities. It is what keeps the business as a going concern. It can be thought of as the amount of fuel a vehicle needs to go one more mile. In that sense, it stands to reason that the lower the working capital required, the better. That is indeed the case. In fact, it is best when the working capital requirement is actually a negative number—more on this point later.

Working capital optimization is a focused approach to improve cash flow from internal and external sources. It is accomplished through an analysis of critical business processes, such as accounts receivable, accounts payable, procurement, and treasury operations. Information obtained from this analysis can help to identify cash recovery opportunities throughout the organization. It can also provide the basis for developing strategies to improve financial performance metrics by minimizing financing costs and reducing dependency on external funding. A positive cash flow achieved through working capital optimization enables companies to meet current and long-term financial obligations. Without positive cash flow, companies must rely on lines of credit and other short-term borrowing, which further increase the cost of doing business. Working capital optimization improves cash flow, thereby minimizing reliance on lines of credit and other short-term borrowing.

Strictly defined,

$$\text{Working capital} = C + AR + I - (AP + D + AE)$$

where:

C = cash and cash equivalents
AR = accounts receivable
I = inventory
AP = accounts payable
D = short-term debt (including current portion of long-term debt)
AE = accrued expenses (including taxes and wages)

51

Focusing on working capital is very important primarily due to two very fundamental concerns of any business enterprise: liquidity and growth.

The relationship between working capital and liquidity is often seen in the form of the various liquidity ratios. One of the most commonly used liquidity ratio is the current ratio:

Current ratio = Current assets/Current liabilities

This ratio is considered good when it is above 1, and its level of "goodness" is quite industry dependent. However, when this ratio gets close to 1, it is a sign of trouble. This low level indicates that there is not enough cash coming in from short-term assets to pay for the short-term liabilities. The short-term assets are cash and cash equivalents, accounts receivable, and inventory. If not enough of these are coming in, we know that the company does not have enough cash coming in during the current year. If this ratio falls below 1, it is an emergency signal regardless of how much cash is available in the bank. A current ratio of below 1 indicates that the business will run out of cash within the year, as it will not have enough cash on hand or coming in from short-term assets to pay for its short-term liabilities (which include accounts payable, accrued expenses, and short-term portion of long-term debt). This ratio also can be too high, indicating that the business is sitting on too much idle cash instead of making value-creating investments. As an example, Microsoft Corporation had a cash reserve of $60 billion in 2004 when it announced a one-time dividend of $32 billion to its shareholders. The decision to pay a dividend in this fashion is often a signal that, at that time, management could not find a project within the company that would make a better investment for its shareholders. The other reason, which did not apply to Microsoft, would be to ward off any forced takeover of a public firm if its stock price is beaten down while it has an unusually high cash reserve. In that case, treasury usually makes the decision to buy back shares of the firm as what is called treasury stock.

The other liquidity ratio most commonly used is very similar to the current ratio and is called the quick ratio:

Quick ratio = (Current assets − Inventory)/Current liabilities

This ratio is called the *acid test*. It is the same as the current ratio except inventory is deducted from current assets in the numerator. The reason for this deduction is that inventory is not as liquid as cash or receivables. Whereas receivables can be converted into cash usually within 30 to 60 days as part of the normal business process, inventory-to-cash conversion is not so predictable. In addition, the value of inventory in case of liquidation is not the same as its book value. This ratio shows how quickly a business can pay off its short-term obligations without having to sell its inventory. Lenders of a business watch this ratio very closely.

Working capital is defined by general ledger accounts whose balances determine these key liquidity ratios such as:

- Current Ratio
- Quick Ratio
- Sales/Receivables Ratio
- Day's Receivable Ratio
- Cost of Sales/Inventory Ratio
- Day's Inventory Ratio
- Cost of Sales/Payables Ratio
- Day's Payables Ratio
- Sales/Working Capital Ratio

Since maintaining sufficient liquidity is a fundamental requirement for the viability of any business, managing these working capital accounts is critical to the survival and growth of a business enterprise. Although some tactical maneuvers and some illegal accounting manipulations might make the ratios look healthy for a short time, the true drivers for business success lie within the processes that cause changes to these accounts through normal business transactions.

As we have seen, working capital includes components that drive these ratios and provides a means for managing them in a way that ensures sufficient liquidity for the business enterprise. Next, we see how working capital relates to the growth of a business.

In Chapter 1, we discussed various measures of profitability. Among these, one of the most commonly understood and talked about is the net profit margin, the so-called *bottom line*:

Net profit margin = Net income/Revenue = NI/R

where

NI = net income
R = revenue

Intuitively, we understand that a business that continues to lose money cannot last long. So, if the net profit (net income) is negative, the only way the business can continue operations is through further injection of capital in the form of equity or debt. Clearly, this capital injection cannot continue indefinitely. Eventually, any viable business is expected to sustain itself and grow from within, through retained earnings, which originate in the profits that the business earns from its normal operations. Let's now see how net profit margin is related to the growth of a business.

In corporate finance, the concept of sustainable growth rate is well understood. It is defined as the maximum rate at which a business can grow revenue without having to invest new capital through equity or debt. A rate of growth higher than this rate can be achieved only for a relatively short period of time; it is not sustainable. In terms of profitability ratios, the return on equity (ROE) ratio indicates the maximum sustainable growth rate that can be achieved. The maximum rate would be that where all of the retained earnings are used for growth. Anything higher than that would require investment of capital. Therefore, the sustainable growth rate can be estimated as:

Sustainable growth rate = $\text{ROE} \times (1 - \text{Dividend Payout Ratio})$

In this equation, if the business pays out no dividends, as in the case of Microsoft for a long time, it can use 100% of retained earnings for growth. In order to grow faster, the company would have to invest more equity capital or increase its financial leverage; either decision would alter its capital structure. If incremental financial leverage is not a viable option (perhaps due to existing debt covenants or unfavorable conditions in the financial markets, as existed between 2007 and 2009), it would have to raise equity capital if possible. As sales growth is not necessarily profitable, in order to grow equity through retained earnings rather than issue it through sale of additional shares, the business would need its ROE to be positive. This control over ROE is related to effective and efficient working capital management.

Expanding the earlier formula into its component parts, we can rewrite it in this way:

$$SGR = (NPM \times (1 - d) \times [1 + (D/E)]/ \\ (A/S - (NPM \times (1 - d) \times [1 + (D/E)])$$

where:

SGR = sustainable growth rate
NPM = net profit margin
d = dividend payout ratio

D/E = debt-to-equity ratio

A/S = asset turnover ratio = Total assets/Revenue

In this form of the equation, sustainable growth rate is the highest revenue growth rate a business can achieve while still maintaining its targets for these financial controls:

- Debt-to-equity ratio
- Dividend payout ratio
- Asset turnover ratio

If the sustainable growth rate is exceeded, one or more of these financial controls targets will have to be changed through a policy decision. Such changes may or may not be desirable. If growth is not managed and SGR is ignored, trouble may ensue in the form of dried-up liquidity. There are ample examples of this phenomenon from the dot-com era. Even very successful companies with highly talented management forget this fundamental law of finance at times and suffer adverse consequences. Dell Computer Corporation made this mistake and learned its lesson.[2]

The only control variable for managing the sustainable growth rate that does not pertain to financial policy decisions is the net profit margin. To achieve a higher sustainable growth rate while maintaining the target financial policy controls, a firm must increase its NPM. The increase in NPM generates cash as part of retained earnings, which offsets the increase in liabilities created to support growth. This is reflected in the working capital equation components: AR, AP, Inventory (I), and accrued expenses (AE). The extra cash "asset" generated will support the additional AP and AE "liabilities." The way to achieve this cash lies in optimizing the working capital processes to reduce end-to-end process costs and cycle times.

Doing this results in an increased NPM. This higher net profit margin can then support a higher sustainable growth rate.

A related measure and mechanism for controlling liquidity is the cash conversion cycle (CCC), the time lapsed between paying the suppliers for inventory and collecting from the customer for a sale. The shorter the CCC, better the cash flow and the ability to manage liquidity and cash positioning. The CCC is composed of these metrics:

$$CCC = DIO + DSO - DPO$$

where:

DIO = days inventory outstanding
DSO = days sales outstanding
DPO = days payables outstanding

With regard to CCC there are three basic management objectives:

1. Extend DPO as far out as possible while taking all desired cash discounts and not adversely affecting the firm's credit rating.
2. Shorten DSO without negatively affecting sales volume or alienating customers.
3. Shorten DIO while not causing stock outs.

The cost of the CCC can be measured accurately using net present value (NPV) techniques. This cost is equal to the NPV of cash inflows minus the NPV of cash outflows. For example, at a 12% cost of capital, the cost of financing a 45-day CCC for $100 million in annual sales = $45 \times (100{,}000{,}000 \times 0.12/365)$ = $1,479,452. In this case, shortening the CCC by one day is worth $32,876.

The three core processes that affect these CCC components are:

- Purchasing: DIO
- Accounts receivable: DSO
- Accounts payable: DPO

In order for the treasury group to do an effective job of maintaining sufficient liquidity while minimizing the level of idle cash assets, it must have control over and visibility into these core processes and the transactions they execute.

A fresh look at well-established business paradigms is necessary to see how nontraditional sources of capital can be leveraged to fund operations and fuel the growth of a business. Dell challenged the prevailing philosophy of investing in working capital and realized the tremendous advantage it could gain by reengineering and streamlining its product delivery platform. It would use the customer payments received in advance of product shipment to fund some of its working capital needs. Doing this required creating a direct sales capability that Dell did not have at that time. Management, realizing that the value of building this capability would create a strategic advantage that well justified the cost and risk, went ahead. This bold and insightful move catapulted Dell ahead of its competitors, such as HP, delivering annual sales growth rates of over 52%.

This "free capital" enabled Dell to capture a greater market share through aggressive pricing strategies. Achieving this type of CCC required:

- Reducing days inventory
- Reducing days receivables
- Lengthening days payables

Figure 3.2 shows the CCC and its components.

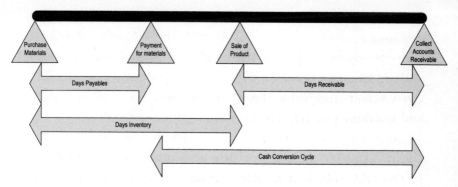

FIGURE 3.2 Cash Conversion Cycle

Working Capital Processes

The working capital processes are the core components of the financial back office. All cash inflows and outflows take place through them as does as the management of the financial structure and procurement of good and services, for both direct and indirect spending. Looking at each process at a high level will set the stage for Chapters 5 though 8, where each process will be studied in detail along with best practices for optimizing each one.

Accounts Receivable

For the vast majority of small and medium business enterprises in the United States, 60% of the working capital is tied up in accounts receivable. It is one of the three largest tangible assets for 75% of the companies in the United States. The purpose of the accounts receivable function is to manage this asset effectively and efficiently.

The basic purpose of accounting is to ensure that a business entity has an accurate picture of its financial condition at all times. Accounts receivable contributes to this accuracy in several ways. One of its primary tasks is the billing of customers for services or goods rendered. Typically, it is accounts receivable that keeps up with the billing information and customized billing needs of clients. Along with creating and distributing invoices to customers, accounts receivable often is responsible for receiving payments on those invoices and making sure the payments are applied correctly.

Accounts receivable also works closely with the treasury and accounts payable arm of the accounting process. Just as clients are expected to pay for goods and services rendered, the company is expected to pay outstanding invoices to vendors in a timely manner. Accounts receivable supports accounts payable in this function by making sure information about the amount of usable revenue is available and accurate. With that data available, accounts payable can schedule and make payments on behalf of the company.

Accounts Payable

Accounts payable is the obligation that a business owes to its creditors for buying goods or services. That is, it is the unpaid invoices, bills, or statements for goods or services rendered by outside contractors, vendors, or suppliers.

The term "accounts payable" (A/P) also is used to refer to the function within an organization's accounting department that manages these payments. The A/P function often oversees a variety of tasks, which may include authorizing purchase orders, collecting credit card receipts, organizing account withdrawals, keeping the general ledger, and auditing expense reports.

The role of the A/P function is a crucial one: Paying bills on time and according to the specific terms and conditions can affect company credit ratings and ultimately business relationships.

Procurement

At the most basic level, procurement entails four steps that are used in the acquisition of goods and services. From this perspective, all consumers participate in the process of procurement. Whether we are procuring items for business or for the home, we all follow progressive steps as we work toward procuring those items that we desire. These steps are:

- Recognition of a need
- Definition of what would satisfy the need
- Evaluation of potential suppliers of the solution
- Taking possession of the desired solution

The first step in the process of procurement is the recognition that there is a need or want for a particular good or service. Before there is a chance for the acquisition of goods, there has to be the desire actually to gain possession of something in particular. Without recognizing the want or need, there is no reason to pursue any of the steps that ultimately lead to a purchase. In short, if there is no desire, there will be no procurement.

Once the need or want has been recognized, it is important to qualify the specifics of what will lead to satisfaction. For example, the want or need may be a new house. Further thought may yield the fact that a one-story dwelling would be the most effective and useful type. Next it is a matter of determining what features are desired as well as determining an approximate amount of money that the consumer is willing to pay for the house. With a solid vision of what is desired, it is possible to move on to the third step in the process of procurement.

The third step involves the evaluation of potential suppliers. This will involve getting to know more about vendors who can supply goods or services that will meet all the specifications, including the price range. Doing this may involve taking bids on a project, negotiating prices, or accepting proposals. Over time, one or two suppliers are likely to stand out from all other vendors. Once the final decision is made between the two remaining suppliers, the time has arrived to move on to the final stage of the procurement process.

The fourth step involves taking possession of the desired good or service, ensuring that the item is in compliance with all the claims made by the supplier, and rendering payment according to the terms worked out with the supplier. In some cases, it may be possible to engage in the acquisition of services and goods prior to supplying payment. At other times, payment may be necessary before taking possession. With both scenarios, the consumer usually has a short period during which it is possible to reverse the acquisition and move on to another option.

One of the basic rules of procurement is that, in the end, it is important to think in terms of the total cost of ownership. This includes not only the purchase price but also time and resources that are expended in the pursuit of the ownership. By understanding the steps involved with procurement, it is possible to get a better understanding of the real cost involved with attaining any good or service.

Treasury Operations

With the evolution of the world economy, the resources for value creation are changing from manufacturing plant and assembly workers to information and financial capital. As this transformation occurs, the responsibilities of the financial manager in the treasury function have become considerably more than managing the cost of capital, determining that accounting entries are correct, and calculating if there are adequate bank balances to cover today's check clearings. The job requires an intimate knowledge of the core elements of the business enterprise regardless of the financial manager's functional assignment in addition to working with other senior managers to optimize operational processes.

The responsibilities of a treasury function in today's corporation include:

- Cash and working capital management
- Short-, medium-, and long-term financing
- Short-, medium-, and long-term investing
- Cash flow forecasting
- Banking relationships management
- Management reporting
- Controls and risk management
- Tax reporting and payment
- Accounting for financial instruments
- Interest rate exposure management
- Foreign current exposure management
- Calculating daily cash position
- Initiating and approving internal and external funds transfers

In order to perform this myriad of tasks, today's treasury function cannot operate in a silo as it did in the Old Economy. The Old Economy being the state of the globally compartmentalized marketplace where commerce was dominated by brick and mortar business enterprises and their suppliers. Treasury today operates at the junction of core processes where two of the most vital resources of the enterprise connect: capital and information. This makes treasury vital to achieving the fundamental corporate goal: to maximize return on equity and shareholder value. Today's treasury functions at the core of the processes that affect the working capital of the organization are shown in Figure 3.3.

Case Study

A $2.5 billion-plus revenue organization in the United States wanted to expand its operations into Canada and Mexico. The primary business it was engaged in was retail pawn shops. The opportunity was based on its deep penetration into the cash store and pawn shop market. The company was cash rich and did not want to increase its financial leverage to support the expansion.

An analysis of its financial structure and core financial processes revealed that it was operating with a significant amount of slack in working capital. It had a tremendous amount of cash trapped in its working capital due to the cash-rich nature of its operations and the lack of visibility into the end-to-end operating cycle from a treasury perspective.

It successfully implemented a financial back-office optimization program that included these components:

- Purchasing card (P-card) program to reduce accounts payable transaction volume
- E-invoicing (Electronic Invoicing) to reduce manual work in A/P and reduce cycle times
- ePayables (Electronic Payables) to reduce the cost for A/P disbursements
- Treasury platform to automate bank statement reconciliation and banking fees analysis

Within the first year of going live with these initiatives, the organization realized a cost savings of over $12 million. These savings were permanent and allowed the redeployment of resources to other higher-value tasks.

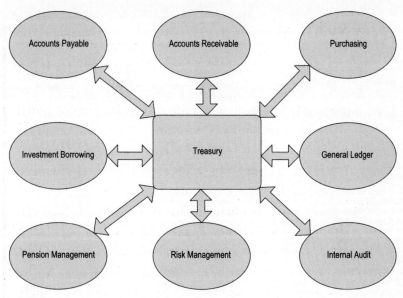

FIGURE 3.3 Treasury Interfaces

Conclusion

The financial supply chain is all about information, and information has a very brief useful life in a business context. When we understand this fact and recognize the increasingly critical role of the financial supply chain in today's global commerce arena, we realize that slow-moving, error-prone, paper-based processes have no room in today's financial supply chain. Indeed, the very existence of paper in any of the core working capital processes is a certain sign of significant loss of value within the organization resulting in a definite competitive disadvantage.

Long-term profitability is not just about being concerned about the cash flow and margins of the own organization any longer. We are living in an age where the strength of a business enterprise is defined by the strength of its supply chain—and that includes the financial supply chain. The days of

TABLE 3.1 Core FSC Optimization Initiatives, Their Costs, and ROI

Function	Process/Issue	Initiative	Effort (low, med, high)	ROI (low, med, high)
Accounts Payable				
	Invoice receipt	Use e-Invoicing network	M	H
	Invoice approval	Use purchase order invoices for straight-through processing or work flow automation for non–purchase order	M	H
	Invoice payment	Use P-card and ePayables to reduce disbursement. costs	L	H
	Invoice errors	Use Evaluated Receipt Settlement to minimize errors	M	M
Procurement				
	Spend management	Use eProcurement	M	H
	Terms optimization	Rationalize vendor master	L	H
	Discount management	Use e-invoicing for incoming invoices	M	H

TABLE 3.1 *(Continued)*

Function	Process/Issue	Initiative	Effort (low, med, high)	ROI (low, med, high)
Accounts Receivable				
	Billing	Use e-invoicing network	L	H
	Payment processing	Use ePayables	L	M
	Managing discounts and fees	Use purchase order flip	L	M
	Collection	Use dynamic discounting	L	H
Treasury				
	Leverage banking relationships	Use P-card	L	H
	Cash management	Use ePayables	M	H
	Monitor and optimize banking fees, automate statement reconciliation	Automate and integrate information in AP, AR, procurement; use a treasury automation platform	M	M
	Cash management	Use receivables exchange	L	H

playing cost-shifting games with upstream and downstream value chain partners are over. To win today and tomorrow, leading organizations will have to think and act win-win with these partners.

To enable leaders to have win-win conversations with their counterparts and to make informed decisions, integration and standardization of information channels is critical. To this end, Table 3.1 lists the core financial supply chain processes along with optimization initiatives that can form the foundation for a road map for transformation. The relative effort and cost column should help in prioritizing the initiatives to suit the needs and constraints of the individual organization.

The "Effort" and "ROI" columns indicate the relative value from the initiative and the relative effort (time, resources, money) required to gain that value as compared to other initiatives. Actual numbers for both would depend on several factors, including:

- Current state of process sophistication and optimization
- Organizational culture in the context of change management
- Quality of skills and experience of the people involved in the end-to-end transformation effort

Notes

1. www.indexmundi.com.
2. www.strategy-business.com/press/16635507/9571.

CHAPTER 4

Platform for Execution: A System for Maximizing Profits

The first rule of any technology used in a business is that automation applied to an efficient operation will magnify the efficiency. The second is that automation applied to an inefficient operation will magnify the inefficiency.

—Bill Gates

Strictly defined, a platform for execution is comprised of the digitized core processes of a business enterprise. It enables management to focus on strategic issues and opportunities instead of managing routine tasks. It provides uniformity, transparency, and velocity to the critical information necessary for making decisions. A platform for execution is something no business can do without and few businesses possess.

Henry Ford used an assembly line to build automobiles and created history. He revolutionized the *process* for making automobiles. Ford is famous for saying "Any customer can have a car painted any color that he wants so long as it is black." If you think carefully, the most important part of this quote is the first half, which suggests that the common person is able to afford an automobile for the first time in history. Ford realized intuitively that the longer it took to execute a process, such as building an automobile, the greater the probability of variation within the tasks of the process. And now as we know from the science and practice of lean and six sigma, as advanced by Toyota Motor Company and other Japanese manufacturers, the combination of variation and delay in a process does indeed drive up the total cost of the process execution. By eliminating variation and specializing the tasks, Ford was able to leapfrog his competition and capture tremendous market share. What was his key advantage? Lower operating costs as compared to the rest of the industry. What gave him this key advantage? A platform for execution: the assembly line.

A process is a sequence of specific tasks executed in a certain order where each task has certain inputs and one or more outputs. Ford took all the various processes that were involved in making an automobile and laid them out in a manner such that the sequence of tasks within each process was logical. He then arranged the processes in a manner that allowed the optimization of the biggest cost component involved in making an automobile: human labor. The next step was to drive out variation from the entire set of processes, and this was achieved by creating the assembly line. What we just described is the core definition of a platform for execution: a set of core processes that are streamlined, automated, and standardized. Each Ford automobile was made in exactly the same way with no variation from the standards of its time. This reduction in process variation and increase in task speed due to specialization resulted in an 8 to 1 increase in production while using less labor.

A successful business enterprise first develops an *operating model* on the revenue-facing side and then applies innovation and automation to gain advantage over its competitors to capture market share. The typical operating model of a business enterprise is configured as shown in Figure 4.1.

70

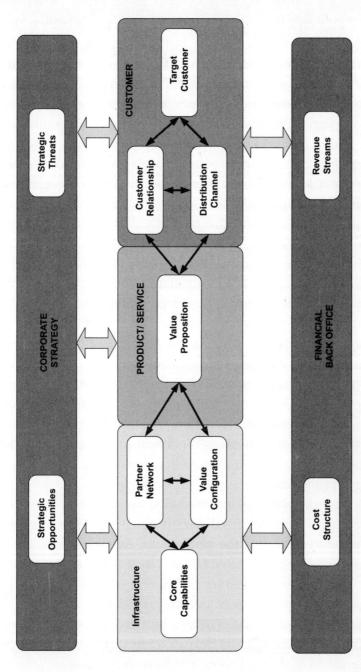

FIGURE 4.1 Generic Operating Model

71

What is equally important for maximum profitability is that the operating model creates a platform for execution in the financial back office. In the context of financial supply chain, a platform for execution consists of the streamlined, automated, integrated, and standardized financial processes related to core working capital, including accounts receivable, accounts payable, purchasing, and treasury. With the exception of business enterprises that are truly considered world-class operations front to back, most businesses do not put forth the effort to optimize their financial back office. The financial back office is usually a collection of stovepipe solutions that exist in functional silos and have little strategic value. They are put in place for the purpose of managing transactions and not geared toward a holistic approach for maximum profitability. This state of affairs is primarily driven by the prevalent mind-set that the financial back office is a cost center, and, therefore, the less spent on it the better. Without an efficient and effective platform for execution, the management talent is unnecessarily consumed by routine activities that can and should be handled without their involvement. When management time is spent on monitoring transactional activities, the value-added work of analytical thinking and planning critical to the growth of the business suffers. The business suffers, as is seen in less-than-optimal profitability.

A generic platform for execution for the financial back office is shown in Figure 4.2. This diagram should not be misconstrued to mean that the platform for execution is an information technology (IT) concern or that it is driven by IT. On the contrary, it is the business value that is the key driver for the platform for execution. As we go through the next few sections and explore the details of business process engineering and optimization, it will become clear that IT is the *enabler* of the platform for execution, *not* its driver or owner.

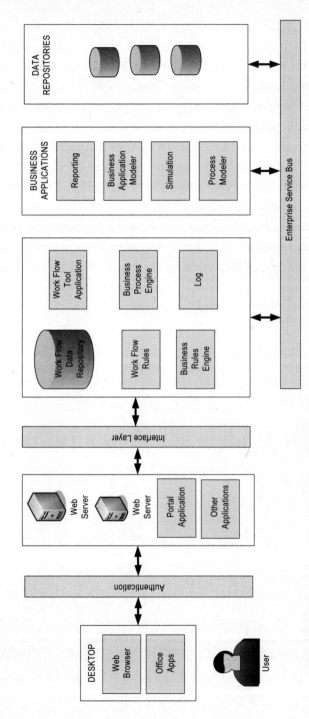

FIGURE 4.2 Generic Financial Back-Office Platform for Execution

First and foremost, we must define, design, and engineer the core financial back-office processes that will be digitized in the platform for execution. In addition, a key objective of this design should be to build flexibility into these processes with the understanding that process optimization is not a one-time effort. World-class business enterprises engage in continuous monitoring and optimization of their financial back-office platform for execution to sustain maximum profitability. This agility gives the business tremendous advantage in the face of strategic opportunities and threats.

In the rest of this chapter, we go through each step needed for creating a *financial back-office platform for execution for maximum profitability*.

Process Benchmarking

In the story of *Alice's Adventures in Wonderland* by Lewis Carroll, one very insightful passage is when Alice comes to a fork in the road and sees the Cheshire Cat up in a tree:

> *"Would you tell me, please, which way I ought to go from here?" said Alice.*
> *"That depends a good deal on where you want to get to," said the Cat.*
> *"I don't much care where ..." said Alice.*
> *"Then it doesn't matter which way you go," said the Cat.*

So it is with a business process. We must know where we are today and where we want to be in order to devise a plan of action to get there. Knowing the current state of a process that defines where we are today and having some idea of the desired target state enables us to create a road map of how to get to the desired target state. Defining the two states requires very specific and rather different kinds of tasks and expertise. To understand where we are starting from, we must begin by measuring the end-to-end process as it exists at present. This includes all aspects of the process: tasks, task sequences and dependencies, lead times, idle times, work-in-process times, error rates, throughput, input, output, variations, and costs.

The second part is knowing where to go. A well-tested starting point is comparing the processes of an organization to peers in the industry and across industries. This is called benchmarking. Knowing what others have achieved is a very good starting point, but it should not necessarily be the end point. Unfortunately, a great many process improvement initiatives leave a lot of potential value on the table by stopping at benchmarking and simply achieving parity with the peers. What is state of the art today will most definitely not be state of the art tomorrow. Change is the only constant. As such, even best practices have a limited time frame for being best practices. Unless a business is satisfied with being a laggard in this respect and accepts that real financial value will be lost due to inefficiency, it is imperative to go to the next step of process optimization. After all, just because your peers are doing things a certain way does not mean that there isn't a better way. That is exactly what Ford did and made history. Imagine what would have happened, or not happened, had Ford simply stopped at benchmarking his automobile production processes against his peers in the industry. In fact, it is claimed that the whole idea of the assembly line for the automobile came to Ford from an entirely different and unrelated industry—a strong case for benchmarking outside the industry.[1]

Process benchmarking is not a novel idea. Most people are at least familiar with the concept, and quite a few business enterprises actually engage in what they think is process benchmarking. A typical financial back-office process benchmarking initiative goes something like this:

1. Concern is raised by senior management about the efficiency of a process.
2. A project is initiated, and the team is organized with members from the functional area (process owners) and possibly some members from IT.
3. The team guesstimates process time and cost in this way:
   - Divide total full-time equivalent (FTE) time allocated to the process per week according to the departmental budget by the total number of transactions processed per week to get the process cycle time.
   - Divide the weekly budgeted costs for the FTEs assigned to the process by the weekly number of transactions processed to get the cost per transaction.
4. The team collects industry average data for the process in terms of total process time, number of units per period of measurement, and total number of people engaged in the process.
5. The team compares the data captured in steps 3 and 4 to determine whether the process is efficient enough or not.
6. If the process is deemed inefficient, the team looks for best practices to improve the efficiency.

What shortcomings do we notice in this approach? One major shortcoming is that it is unscientific. Based on the results produced by an approach similar to this, which is all too common, it is no wonder that most senior management teams have no stomach for "process optimization" initiatives. They worry more about the revenue-enhancing initiatives in an effort to increase profits. But let's not forget that not all growth is desirable from a shareholder value point of view. Not only that, managers often forget the relationship among revenue, cost, and profit. Let's use a simple example to understand this relationship.

Say that a business is operating on a 5% net profit margin (NPM). This implies that every $20 of revenue contributes $1 to profit:

$$\$20 \times 0.05 = \$1$$

The revenue to profit ratio is $20:1$.

The ratio of cost to profit is $1:1$. Every dollar in cost directly adds to or reduces profit.

For this business, an annual reduction of $500,000 through financial back-office optimization would be equivalent to an increase in annual revenue of $10 million. Keep in mind also that while the cost reduction based on business process optimization is permanent and independent of the economy, competition, customers, and suppliers, the equivalent annual revenue increase is not permanent and depends heavily on the economy, competition, customers, and suppliers.

At most organizations, the back-office processes are not *engineered*; rather, they have evolved over time. A historically long-standing process is used, and the process changes are induced by a haphazard sequence of events, such as a regulatory change or the availability of a point technology solution. Even in organizations with very sophisticated and impressively well-engineered production processes, the back-office processes are left to chance. It is no wonder then that there is such a tremendous amount of waste in the financial supply chain, which depends on the financial back-office processes in order to function. The efficiency of the financial supply chain is directly related to the efficiency of the financial back-office processes. Leaving these processes to chance is a significant and tragic waste of corporate value that is completely avoidable with current process engineering principles and technologies for process execution and information availability.

Process engineering is an exercise in process analysis and design. The body of knowledge that is part of the lean methodology has enabled tremendous improvements in process engineering capabilities. The value of this truly becomes evident when you consider the back-office processes that really constitute a services business within a business. It has been calculated that work that adds no value in the customers' eyes typically comprises 50% of the total cost of services work. This understanding has led to the focus on optimizing the financial supply chain by driving efficiencies in the financial back-office functions. With the global economic downturn of 2007 that is still with us today, more and more businesses are looking within for opportunities—not only to enhance profitability but to survive. This effort for process optimization is an ongoing activity, as shown in Figure 4.3.

Lean offers a very effective tool for capturing the current state a time value map (TVM). Time-value mapping is an exercise in which each task or stage of a process is classified and measured. The classification falls into one of three categories:

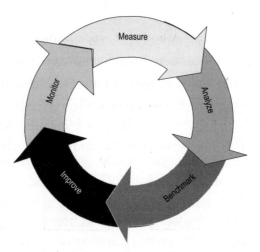

FIGURE 4.3 Continuous Process Optimization

1. Value added: The customer would pay for its output.
2. Business non–value added: The customer would not pay for the output but the task is needed for accounting, compliance, regulatory purposes, and so on.
3. Non–value added: The customer will not pay for the output, and it is not required for business reasons.

Having classified the tasks and steps in the process, we next measure the process. The dimensions of measurement include lead time, work-in-process time, and wait time for each task. This results in a measure of the efficiency of the entire process. An example of a purchase order process value stream map is shown in Figure 4.4.

Process efficiency is defined in terms of the time spent on value-creating activities and total lead time. In Figure 4.4, the lower part of the timeline shows the productive time in the process while the higher part shows the wait time between process steps. The total timeline depicts the lead time for the entire purchase order process. "Lead time" is defined by Little's Law as:

$$\text{Lead Time} = \text{Amount of work-in-process}/$$
$$\text{Average completion rate}$$

Lead time tells us how long it takes to deliver the product or service from the moment the order is triggered. The way to understand this equation is to interpret it as telling us how long it will take any item of work to be completed (lead time) by

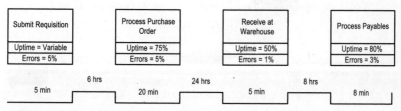

FIGURE 4.4 Purchase Order Process Time Value Map

counting how much work is sitting around waiting to be completed (work in process) and how many things we can complete in each measurement period (average completion rate).

There are two ways to improve the lead time: Either increase the average completion rate (the denominator) or decrease the work in process (the numerator). Usually increasing the average completion rate takes more investment of time and money in the form of additional equipment and human resources. Another way to achieve the same result is to decrease the work in process. In order to accomplish this, the process itself must manage the process input timing. If the preceding step controls the timing of the work that is an input to the process (a push system), then the work in process is not manageable for this process, and variations in lead time will result, all else being equal. If, however, the process controls the timing of its own input (a pull system), given the fixed average completion rate for the process, lead time can be optimized. This is depicted in Figure 4.5.

Let's say that the average completion rate for a production process is 30 units per day. If the input to the process is 60 units per day, then the lead time can be calculated as:

$$\text{Lead Time} = \text{Work in process}/\text{Average completion rate}$$
$$= 60/30 = 2$$

For this process, the lead time is 2 days. Let's say that management wants to reduce the lead time to 1.5 days to better serve the market. In order to achieve this, the work in process would be calculated as:

$$\text{Work in process} = \text{Lead time} \times \text{Average completion rate}$$
$$= 1.5 \times 30 = 45$$

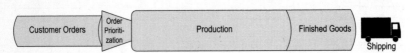

FIGURE 4.5 A Pull System Process

For this process, the work in process would have to be 45 requests per day in order to be able to deliver on the 1.5 days' lead time. Exceeding this rate would only clog the process and increase lead time, which is not desired. A necessary component of this exercise is to devise a system of work prioritization. Usually not all work items are equally important to the enterprise from an economic value or strategic viewpoint; with this in mind, it is a relatively straightforward task to create an order input prioritization system. A production process could, for example, use a method to prioritize the inputs for its pull system on a scale of 1 to 9 for each of these criteria, using odd numbers only:

- Complexity of the order
- Gross profit
- Competitive advantage value

Let's assume that we have three orders that need to be prioritized as shown in Table 4.1. We would first assign a rating on a scale of 1 to 9 for each criterion and then assign multiple the ratings for each order to calculate a total score for each. The orders would then be priority ranked based on the highest total score.

In this example, we would "pull" Order 2 first, then Order 3, and last Order 1. Keep in mind that this prioritization model

TABLE 4.1 Order Prioritization for Pull System

	Order 1	Order 2	Order 3
Complexity (1 = high)	1	5	3
Gross profit (1 = low)	3	7	5
Competitive advantage (1 − low)	9	3	5
Total score	27	105	75
Priority rank (1 = highest)	3	1	2

would be executed continuously as new orders are injected into the order prioritization funnel. This enables the production process to execute at optimal efficiency and minimizes the lead time. One significant caveat to this approach to managing work in process is that it should *not* be applied to customer-facing processes. Since the method does not follow the first-in, first-out principle, it would be very destructive to customer relationships and customer loyalty and the only option to avoid this negative impact would be to focus on the denominator in the equation and add more resources to increase the average completion rate.

The effect of process optimization on business profitability maximization is revealed when we consider these data:

- Service process efficiency typically is 5%, meaning that 95% of the time, the work item is just waiting to be worked on (e.g., invoices, purchase orders, human resource forms).
- The cost of the resources employed in service processes is not based on discrete units of usage; rather it is based on a continuous flow of cost (e.g., FTE cost).

When we combine these two bits of data, it is evident that the longer a service work item waits to be processed, the greater the cost to the organization. The whole thrust of the lean movement is to increase the *velocity* of the process to reduce costs. When combined with six sigma techniques to reduce variations and errors, a business enterprise can achieve world-class performance and cost benefits in its financial back-office processes. To put it in perspective for an organization with an annual cost for the financial back-office processes of $5 million and an overall back-office process efficiency of 10%, if it could achieve 20% process efficiency level, its annual cost savings would be:

$$(20\% - 10\%) \times 95\% \times \$5,000,000 = \$475,000$$

That is a significant amount of cost optimization that would directly add to the return on invested capital (ROIC) and hence shareholder value. This is not a theoretical example; it is just one of the many cases of financial back-office optimization executed by a knowledgeable and experienced team.

The concept of work in process applies to any item that is an output of a business process. For example, in accounts payable, the number of invoices going through the approval may constitute work in process for invoice processing.

Related to the concept of work in process is the wait time. Whenever something is being worked on, there may be another thing that is waiting to be worked on. This is essentially the concept of a queue of work where items enter the queue at one end, get worked on in the middle, and come out the other end as the output of the process.

The measure of process efficiency is based on the percentage of value-added process time (lead time) versus the percentage of waste time. It looks like this in an equation:

Process efficiency = Value-added time/Total lead time

Experience in the field has shown that a process efficiency of less than 10% indicates that the process contains a lot of non–value-added waste. In this context, waste can be costs, time, and work. Such a process would be a prime candidate for optimization and therefore cost reduction.

The primary principles of the lean approach are presented next:

- Any process with less than 10% efficiency is a prime target for optimization.
- Work in process is a key element of waste and must be minimized in order to achieve optimal process efficiency.
- Variation in lead time can be minimized by operating the process on the basis of pull instead of push.

- In a process, 80% of the delay is caused by 20% of the tasks.
- In order to see the waste in a process, we need to use data to manage the process.

Velocity and Cycle Times

In manufacturing as well as in services, lean methodology has proven that the faster a process executes end to end, the lower the defect rate. This may seem counterintuitive at first, but upon reflection in the context of a service process, the logic becomes obvious. As we saw earlier, lead time is affected by the rate of introduction of work into the process—the work in process. If this work introduction is not managed through a pull system, the work items will create a backlog in the process queue. In order to get the work moving through the process queue, the staff will cut corners to keep up with the workload. As the staff is then asked to expedite certain work items due to their high priority, they will leave what they currently are doing and switch to another work item. All this switching and expediting between work items requires additional setup time and adds to the wait time for each work item in the process queue. This back-and-forth refocusing leads to errors and rework, and lead time is increased. The perception is that the staff members are working faster, but the reality is that they are spending a greater percentage of the total cycle time on non–value-added work.

To measure the cycle time (end-to-end execution time) for a process, you need to measure the velocity of the work items at each task in the process. This is best done using TVM as we saw earlier. Not only is it important to capture the time spent doing things, it is even more important to capture the time spent *waiting* to do something. These time traps are value destroyers as they are the biggest contributors to process costs.

Error Rates

Errors in a service process generally are related to human communication deficiencies. Communication deficiencies can take many forms, including data entry errors. In addition, in the context of a service process, error rates also are related to complexity and variation. The higher the complexity level of a work item and the greater the variation between work items, the higher the overall error rates will be. Wherever there is human touch in a process, there are errors that lead to increased rework, work in process, lead times, and therefore cost. Order entry and processing are prime examples of such processes, as are almost all the financial back-office processes. The solution to prevent this waste of valuable capital lies in achieving *straight-through processing (STP)* as much as possible. "Straight-through processing" means that information flows directly from one system to another without human intervention. Any process that is transaction oriented is a prime candidate for STP. This automation of routine tasks elevates the human resources for the value-adding analytical tasks while managing by exception in the area of the transactions.

Complexity

Process complexity is a key driver of errors rates and a process cycle time killer. Complexity has to be measured and minimized at each task level through task simplification and specialization. This is best done with the use of a visual aid by breaking down the entire process into its discrete steps or tasks. After laying out the tasks in a storyboard fashion, you can see which tasks are redundant or non–value added or need to be further broken down into subtasks. This mapping continues until the process has been broken down to the simplest possible meaningful tasks. Simplification and specialization of tasks

TABLE 4.2 Process Optimization Result

Metric	Improvement	Metric	Improvement
Operating margin	47%	Capital turnover	32%
Earnings before interest, tax, depreciation, and amortization	275%	Enterprise value	225%
ROIC	230%	Economic profit	1,150%
Average lead time	42%		
Error rates	51%		

will deliver the maximum velocity at the task level. Now the work begins to reorganize the process by resequencing the tasks to deliver maximum process velocity.

Process Optimization

The value of process optimization can be seen in the results shown in Table 4.2 achieved by one company that used lean six sigma methods for reengineering its financial back-office platform for execution as well as its revenue-facing platform.

Process Automation

A process that has been well engineered using lean six sigma is ready for automation. The primary benefits of automation include:

- Lower transaction costs
- Greater staff productivity
- Consistency in task performance
- Transparency of information

86

One of the biggest mistakes made by businesses of all sizes is that they mistake automation for process engineering. All too often, the jump to implement a technology solution is made without first going through the work of process engineering. It is no surprise then that rate of return on IT investments across industries is abysmal. The process is not the same as the automation solution. Technology vendors in general and enterprise resource planning (ERP) solution vendors in particular will tell us that their particular solutions incorporate "best practices out of the box"; thus, there is no need to spend time reengineering the process. There are two problems with this claim:

1. As we discussed earlier, best practices have a limited life—things change.
2. The typical implementation time frame of an ERP system is 12 to 18 months.

These two facts do not mesh with vendor claims when you consider the time between major releases of these very expensive software platforms. If they truly embody so-called best practices, why is there a huge consulting industry built around customizing these platforms as part of implementation?

The rational approach to automation of a business process follows these three steps:

1. Engineer the process using lean six sigma methodologies.
2. Define business rules that facilitate dynamic control of the process in the future.
3. Select an automation solution that best executes the process as designed and facilitates the execution and configuration of the business rules to accommodate the process as is and its changes in the future.

In the financial back office, many processes are still manual or utilize less-than-optimal point solutions. Some examples of these manual processes include:

Accounts Payable
- Invoice receipt and approval
- Vendor payments
- Vendor payment inquiry and dispute resolution

Accounts Receivable
- Invoice creation
- Payment application

Treasury
- Cash forecasting

Purchasing
- Purchase request initiation and approval
- Purchase order generation and delivery

Process Integration

Once the individual processes have been engineered for optimal efficiency and automated to ensure consistency, the next step toward creating a platform for execution is to integrate these financial back-office processes. Information that exists in silo repositories in most organizations does not deliver the value necessary to survive and thrive today. As an example, it does not help the treasury function in creating reliable cash position forecasts if the data for accounts receivable and accounts payable are not readily available. The effort and, therefore, cost involved in pulling the data together through a multitude of reports and spreadsheets, not to mention the possibility and existence of errors, create no value for the enterprise. The information critical to managing liquidity and optimizing investments and capital needs should be readily available at negligible incremental cost. This is what process integration in the financial back-office delivers.

Once again, we should be clear about the role and value ERP platforms provide in this regard. These systems have been around for quite some time. Although they provide good value in the areas they were designed for, they leave much to be desired in the areas where they have developed basic capabilities just to be able to play in the market. This approach of providing basic capabilities may make perfect sense for the vendor in support of its business objectives, but it provides little or no value for the customer. As an example, while most ERP platforms provide an A/P module, such modules do not provide any visibility into the invoice pipeline throughout the invoice life cycle. Some of these platforms are beginning to provide limited capabilities in this regard, there is still much to be desired. ERP systems are little more than massive databases with business-specific applications built on top. They are good for transactional information storage and retrieval. However, at this time they are not good at supporting the end-to-end automation of an entire process. This is the domain of process work flow automation and is the key to achieving an optimal process.

Process Standardization

Once the financial back-office processes have been engineered, automated, and integrated, it is time to ensure that the investments made in these steps are protected by eliminating the possibility of any deviation from them. In this regard, we need a combination of security, business rules, and business policy. The first two are provided directly by a platform for execution through its enabling technology capabilities. The third component is the responsibility of senior management. Without the active support of the senior management, rogue behavior will continue and cause value-destroying deviations from the processes.

An example of this standardization will illustrate the point. Let's say that we have process for purchasing office supplies within our platform for execution. The process utilizes a procurement portal as its automation technology underpinning. In such a system, it is common to have a digital catalog of items that have been selected by the purchasing department from preferred vendors at negotiated prices. In order to manage and control corporate-wide spending, it is very important that all purchases be made of from items that are available in the catalog. Let's assume that a particular supply item is not available and that the need is urgent. To accommodate such a situation, a well-designed purchasing platform would have two features:

1. Enable the purchaser to go outside the catalog and make a purchase directly at the vendor's Web site.
2. Alert the purchasing staff of the transaction including the purchaser's name and item purchased. (The purchaser would have to indicate what was not available in the catalog.)

This procedure would allow the purchasing staff to follow up with the purchaser to understand why the item was not purchased through the catalog and add the item to the catalog if required. The key benefit of this flexible approach is twofold: Since people know that an alert notification will be generated, they are less apt to bypass the catalog. Equally important, it enables the purchasing staff to continuously monitor and improve the buying needs of the organization while still adding value by negotiating the best terms for the enterprise.

Figure 4.6 shows what a financial back-office platform for execution looks like at a high level.

90

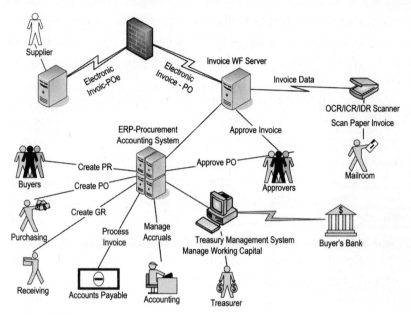

Supplier

Invoice WF Server

Electronic Invoic-POe

Electronic Invoice - PO

Invoice Data

OCR/ICR/IDR Scanner

Scan Paper Invoice

ERP-Procurement Accounting System

Approve Invoice

Mailroom

Create PR

Approve PO

Buyers

Create PO

Approvers

Create GR

Purchasing

Process Invoice

Manage Accruals

Treasury Management System

Manage Working Capital

Buyer's Bank

Receiving

Accounts Payable

Accounting

Treasurer

FIGURE 4.6 Financial Back-Office Platform for Execution

Case Study

A retailer had gone through a number of mergers and acquisitions. Its processes and systems had become a collection of mismatched and often duplicated components. Realizing the value potentially being lost due to inefficient processes and redundant systems, the decision was made to create a road map for streamlining and optimizing the financial back office.

The project team started with a benchmark of the existing processes, systems, and performance metrics. Following the value gap analysis approach, they discovered areas of significant improvement that together constituted what

(Continued)

would become the financial back-office platform for execution for the organization.

After a painstaking effort that lasted about 18 months, a unified platform for execution for the financial back office was implemented that streamlined, automated, integrated, and standardized the core processes in accounts payable, accounts receivable, procurement, and treasury. This enabled the organization to fundamentally reduce costs associated with transactional activities and substantially improved the quality and timeliness of critical information needed for decision making

Conclusion

The greatest benefits of having streamlined core processes that are automated, integrated, and standardized include business agility and cost optimization. Together, these benefits make the performance of the financial back office predictable and reliable to a far greater extent than it is otherwise. Building a financial back-office platform for execution to achieve this goal is an undertaking that requires careful planning by people who understand these key areas at a detailed level:

- The business objectives and process specifics in the as-is state
- Process engineering and lean practices
- State of the art in information technology solutions and vendors
- Working capital implications of process change

The overarching skill that brings the whole effort to fruition is effective change management, a balancing act that requires a thorough knowledge of the financial back office, diplomacy, and effective communications with all stakeholders. Most initiatives in this space that fail have these elements in common:

- Lack of unified support from senior management
- Project team that is ill suited to the task
- Inadequate change management planning and execution

Organizations that have traveled this path to build a financial back-office for execution have reaped the reward of sustainable maximum profitability. They have also found that once they have achieved this goal, their work is not done. They have embraced a culture of continuously monitoring and improving their financial back-office platform for execution, recognizing that state of the art and best practices both have a limited life span.

Now that we know the tremendous benefits to be gained from a financial back-office platform for execution, let's remember one more thing: In the words of Italian author and poet Dante Alighieri, "The secret of getting things done is to act."

Note

1. Robert Lacey, *Ford: The Men and the Machine* (Boston: Little, Brown, 1986).

CHAPTER 5

Optimizing Accounts Payable

Money often costs too much.

—Ralph Waldo Emerson

The trade obligations of a corporation constitute its short-term liabilities. Paying these liabilities in a manner that balances the need for preserving the corporation's credit rating and managing supplier relationships and cash outflows is the responsibility of accounts payable (A/P).

The largest amount of *cash outflow* for almost every business occurs through the A/P function. However, when we look at the level of attention given by senior management to this critical and cash-rich function, we see a glaring discrepancy between what we would expect and what actually exists. Based on data gathered from business enterprises across the country, the A/P staff at most organizations describes their professional state in this way:

- Underappreciated due to being considered a cost center
- Understaffed due to the corporate focus on cost reduction

- Overworked with long days and even weekends
- Want automation but senior management does not want to spend the money on A/P
- Get blamed for late payments
- Constant threat of job loss through outsourcing

In most organizations today, the A/P function remains one of the most manually intensive and inefficient areas within the financial back office. This is no reflection on the hardworking A/P staff; they are responsible for executing the processes as they exist. It does, however, reflect the fact that a serious lack of attention is given to this function—a function that is crucial to effective working capital management and therefore to the liquidity and profitability of the organization.

Although recent cost-cutting efforts have led organizations to greatly reduce A/P staff levels, most still continue to utilize higher levels of temporary staff (temps) to keep up with the workload at period-end and during audits. This does not reflect the situation as it has to be; rather it reflects the fact that insufficient attention has been paid to optimizing this function, which is ripe for delivering immediate and sustainable value to an organization by releasing large amounts of cash tied up in outdated manual processes.

The key metric in A/P that we want to focus on is days payable outstanding (DPO). This metric measures how long it takes the organization to pay the short-term liabilities due to its suppliers. It is calculated in this way:

$$DPO = (\text{Accounts payable/Cost of goods sold}) \times$$
$$\text{Days in calculation period}$$

Typically measured on a quarterly or annual basis, the A/P number from the balance sheet is divided by the cost of goods sold (COGS) number from the income statement. The result is multiplied by 90 for a quarter or 360 for an annual calculation.

The "goodness" of this measure depends on the industry as well as on the negotiated payment terms an organization has with its suppliers. Within an industry, however, DPO is a good indicator of the efficiency of the A/P process for paying its invoices. Although the typical management directive is to extend the DPO as much as possible, this approach has its limits and ramifications in terms of the more obvious supplier relationships and the less obvious supplier prices and service levels.

Implications of A/P Effectiveness

The decision to extend DPO is justified by the desire to hold on to the cash in treasury as long as possible in order to maintain sufficient liquidity and minimize short-term debt costs. Laudable as this goal is, its achievement through an unreasonably long DPO is based on historical reasons that do not exist today. The science of process optimization and the enabling technological solutions make streamlining and automating A/P processes critical to the financial well-being of an organization and its supply chain both very compelling and beneficial.

The key document that A/P processes are built around is the invoice. This document represents the supplier's bill and touches most if not all A/P processes. Traditionally, an invoice has been a paper document that has no standard format. Each supplier sends an invoice with the type and format of invoice data in a fashion that meets its internal systems needs. Sometimes certain information requested by the buyer is included but not always. The process of receiving, validating, confirming authorization for payment, and archiving this critical paper document is wrought with manual labor, errors, and long cycle times. The implications of not optimizing the A/P invoice process are many and significant. Some of the implications with the most impact to an organization's financial performance metrics include:

- Missed early-pay discounts
- Duplicate payments to vendors
- Unwarranted sales and use tax payments
- Unwarranted freight charge payments
- Higher transaction costs

From the viewpoint of internal controls and specifically for a public company that has to comply with the Sarbanes-Oxley (SOX) Act of 2002 (Section 404) in the United States, the implications are serious. Getting the bills paid on time is no longer adequate; items must be recorded in a timely manner and to the appropriate accounts. Otherwise, budgets and financial statements may end up containing incorrect information, leading to issues related to certification and perhaps restatement of financial statements. From a SOX perspective, some the key implications include:

- Unauthorized payments to suppliers
- Fraudulent payments to suppliers
- Controls around payment cards

The root cause of these financial implications lies in the fact that the core document is in paper form that requires the "physical" movement of information contained within it through the entire process. Not only is this costly and inefficient, it also introduces ample opportunity for errors in data entry and often loss of the document itself. Anyone who has looked for a lost invoice when the supplier calls for payment status or when an auditor requests it for transaction testing is well aware of the pain and aggravation caused by this all-too-common an event. On the process efficiency side of things, time delays exist in moving the information along and then validating it at key steps in a process that requires human touch. The resulting long cycle time increases the cost to the paying organization as well as to the supplier whose cash flow is impacted by this delay.

Best Practices

The best practices for A/P from a procedural viewpoint have been well explained in the books *Accounts Payable Best Practices* and *Accounting Best Practices*.[1] The intent here is to focus on the process and automation technology aspects of best practices as they pertain to invoice processing and payment.

Manage Timing and Terms to Maximize Cash Flow

Managing the A/P function in a strategic manner has a measurable impact on the cash flows of a business enterprise. In this context, the role of A/P goes far beyond just paying bills. The velocity of A/P invoice payments determines the levels of cash that can be retained by the business and how much cost is incurred in the form of interest charges and late payment fees. The cost to finance A/P operations must be monitored closely in order to achieve maximum profitability. Doing this requires that the enterprise has in place a system that enforces invoice payment schedules to prevent early payment of obligations and to avoid any late payment charges. This capability enables an organization to negotiate favorable payment terms with select suppliers and take advantage of suppliers' prompt-payment discounts whenever possible. Realizing that A/P is a critical component of cash flow management, leading companies set A/P performance targets that specifically support the cash flow objective. This means making sure that cash outflows from A/P occur at a rate equal to or slower than the rate cash is received.

A business that utilizes this best practice closely monitors certain key performance indicators, such as DPO and A/P turnover. This information enables the ongoing fine-tuning necessary for achieving realistic performance targets.

By enabling the A/P staff to spend less time on transaction processing tasks and more on value-add tasks such as transaction analysis, the organization as a whole reaps tremendous benefits for maximizing profitability. By spending time to analyze expenditure data and the existing contract compliance rates, the A/P function can help the business enterprise implement purchasing strategies that drive cost efficiency. Another area of value-added analysis is prior payment errors, which would lead to recovering funds lost in transactions that were made by mistake. Since A/P has touch points with both purchasing and finance, it is in a position to synchronize the policies of these departments to improve cash flow. Through analysis, A/P can recommend more cost-efficient purchasing strategies that take advantage of prompt payment discounts or maximize float by extending payment into vendor grace periods. An area where A/P can add significant value is cost and disbursement management. By analyzing specific spending patterns, A/P can determine whether the business is maximizing its cash flows.

Automate Invoice and Remittance Processing

A majority of companies waste significant time and money on non-value-add tasks, such as tracking delinquent invoices and manually keying invoice information. By using best practices within the A/P and purchasing functions mentioned, a business enterprise can avoid such delays by leveraging information technology solutions systems to automate or eliminate steps involved in legacy invoice processing. These technologies, listed in increasing level of sophistication, include:

- Digital imaging
- Optical character recognition (OCR), Intelligent Character Recognition(ICR) and workflow automation (WFA)
- Web-based electronic invoicing (e-invoicing)

The use of these technologies along with the corresponding process optimization, together determine the stages of evolution of the A/P function. The Hardstone Group (www. hardstonegroup.com) has defined three distinct stages in this context:

1. **eA/P-1™**

   This stage of A/P is the first step toward a fully optimized A/P function and is characterized by the use of digital imaging at the front-end of the invoice process. The paper invoice document is turned into a digital image through the use of scanning technology and thereafter, the document image is used for approvals and coding and the process utilizes email for workflow. Creating a digital image at the back-end of the process for archival purposes alone does not constitute an eA/P-1 stage function.

2. **eA/P-2™**

   The second stage of A/P optimization uses technologies that convert paper invoice documents into digital information, not just digital images. Leveraging Optimal Character Recognition (OCR) and Intelligent Character Recognition (ICR), the invoice data is digitized and routed for approval and coding using workflow automation software.

3. **eA/P-3™**

   The third stage of A/P optimization represents the state of the art and removes the paper invoice document from the entire process. It uses end-to-end electronic information processing. This is the stage where electronic invoice presentment and payment (EIPP) and straight through processing (STP) combine to deliver the greatest possible efficiency and effectiveness at this time.

From a process perspective, companies that implement best practices in A/P sometimes entirely eliminate the invoice from the procure-to-pay process by using evaluated receipts settlement (ERS). ERS uses an agreement to pay a supplier based on a preapproved blanket purchase order (PO). In this case, the company itself may generate an invoice from the PO and post it for payment. The biggest benefit of this practice is the elimination of the error and delays caused by a mismatch between a supplier-created invoice and the buyer-created PO. It shortens the payment cycle since the settlement process can be kicked off as soon as the buyer confirms that goods or services are received.

If eliminating invoices entirely is not possible, a business enterprise can work with its suppliers to have them provide summary invoicing in order to reduce the number of invoices that have to be processed. Another very powerful tool is a purchasing card (P-card), which helps consolidate all potential invoices from a supplier into one monthly statement. Some banks that provide P-cards offer electronic payment (ePayables) services for paying invoices outside of the P-card transactions (e.g., JP Morgan Chase and Bank of America provide this service). These electronic payment systems automate the disbursement task within the A/P process and enable companies to make their financial back office more efficient while also reducing costs. Movement of funds automatically between trading partners can be achieved with the use of systems such as electronic funds transfer on a designated settlement date at a fraction of the cost of traditional paper checks. Funds also can be transferred through the national electronic payment exchange, the automated clearinghouse (ACH).

The state of the art in payment settlement between trading partners is financial electronic data interchange (FEDI). FEDI is a combination of EDI and ACH. It allows the simultaneous processing of an invoice with the associated payment transfer. FEDI can be used effectively with suppliers to convert to web-based EIPP systems, enabling trading partners to present invoices and pay bills automatically through the same electronic network.

On the accounts receivable (A/R) side, remittance processing optimization efforts focus on shortening the time between a customer's approval for payment of an invoice and the company's receipt of that payment. Once a payment is received in A/R, automated systems accelerate processing, eliminating expensive time lags for reconciling and posting the payment. With automated remittance processing, which typically includes the use of lockboxes and document imaging technology, employee intervention is minimal. The resources freed by automating this process can be directed toward working with customers to collect payment rather than processing paperwork.

Use Evaluated Receipt Settlement to Reduce Errors and Cycle Times

One of the biggest sources of delays in the procure-to-pay (P2P) process is the invoice. This central document that is exchanged between trading partners generates more errors in the process and therefore causes unduly long cycle times than anything else. Over the years, many attempts have been made to address this problem, both from a process and automation technology aspect. However, in the end, this source of errors and anguish to the A/P staff just will not be tamed.

Originally developed by General Motors, evaluated receipt settlement (ERS) is a process for the settlement of goods receipts. Its key benefits include:

- Saving the company time and money
- Preventing invoice variance
- Eliminating non–value-added work (e.g., tasks associated with reconciliation)
- Opportunity cost of capital savings

With the resolution of the legal and accounting implications, ERS use has spread as a means of electronic interchange of financial information. This business process between trading partners enables commerce without invoices. The overall process flows follow eight steps:

1. Buyer and supplier enter into an agreement to use ERS.
2. Supplier provides a catalog of products and prices.
3. Buyer places an order with a PO or a contract number.
4. Supplier delivers an advanced shipping notice (ASN) to the buyer.
5. Supplier ships products per the ASN.
6. Buyer verifies the existence of a PO or contract based on the ASN.
7. Buyer generates a goods receipt.
8. Goods receipt is matched to the PO or the contract to authorize payment.

There are three key things to note about this process that make it valuable for both trading parties from a cycle time and cost-efficiency viewpoint:

1. There is no invoice involved.
2. ASN does not contain price or tax information.
3. Price and terms are determined from the PO or the contract.

Price variance and tax issues are among the leading causes of delays in invoice processing. ERS eliminates both. It also reduces costs for both parties; no longer do they have to create and deliver and receive and process yet another document. The buyer, having received the goods as ordered, does not have to wait for the arrival of an invoice to schedule payment. The net result is a shorter cycle time from order to payment and lower overall process cost. The savings achieved can be reinvested in the business at both ends.

For most organizations, this represents a radical departure from the traditional process and on the surface appears to be too risky even to consider. Looking deeper into ERS, however, shows that it makes a lot of sense, and the apparent risk seems immaterial. This is not to say that ERS is perfect; rather it is a good step in the right direction. The ERS process flow is outlined in Figure 5.1.

From a platform of execution viewpoint, ERS looks like the diagram shown in Figure 5.2.

Leverage Technology for Win-Win Partnerships with Trading Partners

As we have discussed before, the state of process efficiency is seriously lacking in A/P functions across organizations small and large, private and public, for profit and not for profit, and public sector as well as private sector. The fundamental issues in this regard have to do with insufficient understanding of the value that can be released from A/P in the form of cash. This tangible and material value is being used unnecessarily in working capital.

It is common for finance management in business organizations of all sizes to extend the DPO metric. The logic behind this seems reasonable enough on the surface: By extending

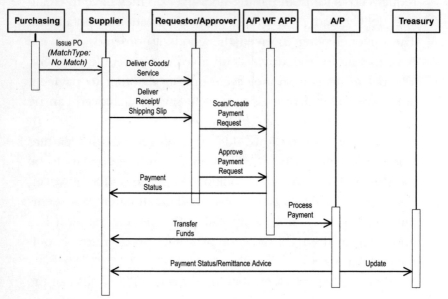

Improving PO Matching Process
Evaluated Receipt Settlement (ERS)
(Sequence Model)

FIGURE 5.1 ERS Process Flow

payables, the company gets the use of "free" money that it owes to its suppliers. Now, we all know that there is no such thing as "free" in business. We may not see the cost, but it is very much there. Let's see if we can uncover the cost of this "free" money in A/P.

Payemlate Corporation has these statistics:

$$\text{Annual spend through A/P} = \$100{,}000{,}000$$
$$\text{Average days payables} = 30 \text{ days}$$
$$\text{Negotiated early-pay discounts} = 2/10 \text{ net } 30$$
$$\% \text{ of annual spend on negotiated discounts} = 30\%$$
$$\text{Weighted average cost of capital (WACC)} = 6\%$$

The negotiated early-pay discount of 2/10 net 30 means that Payemlate can deduct 2% of the total invoice amount if it

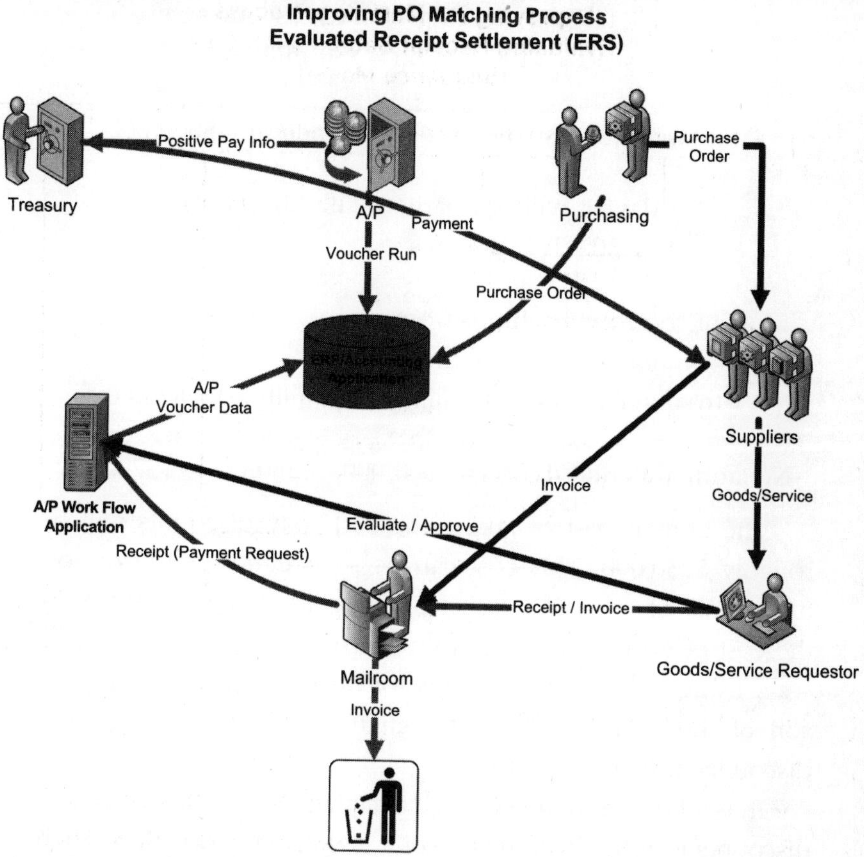

Improving PO Matching Process
Evaluated Receipt Settlement (ERS)

FIGURE 5.2 ERS for PO invoices

pays the invoice within ten days from the invoice date. Otherwise, the entire amount is due by day 30.

In this scenario, Payemlate does not take any of the early-pay discounts, as it wants to hold on to its cash as long as possible by extending its days payables out to 45 days. By doing this, Payemlate expects to improve its working capital, a laudable goal. Let's do a cost-benefit analysis of this financial policy decision for Payemlate:

$$\text{A/P target for taking offered discounts}$$
$$= 30\% \times 100 \text{ million} = \$30 \text{ million}$$

$$\text{Annual discounts value} = 2\% \times 30 \text{ million} = \$600,000$$

$$\text{\# days it will pay early to take discounts}$$
$$= 30 - 10 = 20 \text{ days}$$

$$\text{Cost of "borrowing" funds from}$$
$$\text{its working capital to pay the discounts}$$
$$= (6\%/360) \times 20 \times (100 \text{ million} - 30 \text{ million}) = \$230,000$$

$$\text{Net annual benefit/(cost)} = \$600,000 - \$230,000 = \$370,000$$

The annual cost of taking the early-pay discounts will be roughly $230,000. This cost can be seen either as the opportunity cost of releasing cash from working capital early or as the cost of borrowing funds to make the payment early. Either way, using the WACC provides for apples-to-apples comparison of the options. The net annual benefit from taking the discounts will be $370,000.

It is clear from these numbers that taking the early-pay discounts is in the best interest of Payemlate Corporation. Then why would management in the finance function want to extend its DPO? Not only is this decision financially unfavorable to the enterprise, but it also may lead to an increase in the COGS and indirect expense for the business as suppliers increase their prices to cover the cost of funds they have to borrow for their own working capital needs. Remember, Payemlate's accounts payable is its suppliers' accounts receivable. The answer lies in the fact that if finance looks at the working capital metrics alone, then the decision to extend DPO makes perfect sense. In this case, we are specifically talking about this metric:

$$DWC = DSO + DIO - DPO$$

where

DWC = days working capital
DSO = days sales outstanding
DIO = days inventory outstanding

DWC represents the amount of liquidity required to keep a business's operations running. This is the amount of capital tied up in operations. The target for this number is as close to zero or even negative if the business model allows it. From the equation, we can see that making DPO larger would make the DWC number smaller, all else being equal. However, it should be noted that this is not the only way to make DWC better (smaller). We can achieve the same result by making either DSO or DIO smaller, or both. In reality, though, making DPO larger is most *easily* in the control of an organization and therefore the route taken by most companies to improve the DWC metric. Decreasing DSO requires more effort with today's manual A/R collections processes and depends ultimately on the buyer to make the payment. We will see how this is better managed in Chapter 6, but for now let's just state that new technologies together with the participation of financial institutions enable streamlined procure-to-pay processes that allow better management of the DSO metric.

Organizations do not readily admit that often the real reason behind the extension of DPO is that the A/P cycle time for processing an invoice is so long that a discount could not be taken even if it was desired. When a company does not have the wherewithal to capture an early-pay discount, the most logical thing to do seems to be extending the DPO as much as possible in order to make working capital look better. This path of least resistance, however, masks the costs the organization incurs in other areas as a result of extending DPO. This silo way of looking at financial performance metrics adversely affects the one metric that really matters—return on invested capital—and results in the destruction of shareholder value in the long term.

From a financial supply chain optimization viewpoint, extending DPO is not the best approach. Even when interest rates are high and the gap between the cost and benefit of taking early-pay discounts narrows or disappears, there are better ways for managing working capital and the financial supply chain. These ways do, however, require a fresh and broader perspective. They require that we see the entire financial supply chain in a strategic manner and that we not think of our suppliers as adversaries to be beaten at the game of finance. They require that we seek to drive costs out of the financial supply chain instead of shifting them to our upstream or downstream vendor partners. Of course, this was not possible in the past due to a lack of adequate visibility of the financial supply chain. And whenever there is uncertainty, there is risk, and in finance, risk is a key driver of the cost of capital. In the next section, we see what enabling technologies are available today to allow companies of all sizes to take advantage of better ways of managing their working capital through improved payables management.

An actual medium-size business enterprise with a very manual, paper-intensive A/P function had the metrics as shown in Table 5.1.

The annual cost for processing invoices to the point of getting them ready for payment was $3,960,000. Not included

TABLE 5.1 Metrics for Manual A/P Invoice Processing

Metric	Value
Invoices processed per month	22,000
Full-time equivalent (FTE) count for invoice processing	27
Invoices processed per FTE per year	9,777
Average days invoice ready for payment	42
Cost for invoice ready for payment	$15

in this cost are payment disbursement costs and missed discounts.

This organization had an annual A/P spend of around $60 million. Due to its inability to process invoices in a timely manner, on a conservative estimate, it was missing out on an annual early-pay discount benefit of:

$$50\% \times 60,000,000 \times 2\% = \$600,000$$

Quite a few finance professionals do not want to consider the opportunity cost of missed early-pay discounts as part of a cost-benefit analysis for automating A/P processes, but they do so at the expense of shareholder value. This cost is very real and can be measured in hard dollars. It is understandable where that mind-set comes from; historically the A/P function could not decrease its cycle time for invoice processing so there was no point in looking at this as a tangible benefit. With today's technologies, however, this benefit has become very tangible. It is there for the taking for any organization willing to optimize its A/P operations through process engineering, automation, integration, and standardization. Figure 5.3 depicts the actual environment of this organization before it embarked on A/P process optimization.

Through a careful analysis of its current situation and the overall objectives of the organization for improving its working capital, it was determined that optimizing the A/P processes around invoice payment would deliver a substantial return on investment (ROI). An objective analysis using lean six sigma tools and methodology revealed that the three key drivers of this ROI objective were:

1. Speed of invoice approval
2. Reduction in coding errors
3. Removal of small-dollar invoices from the process

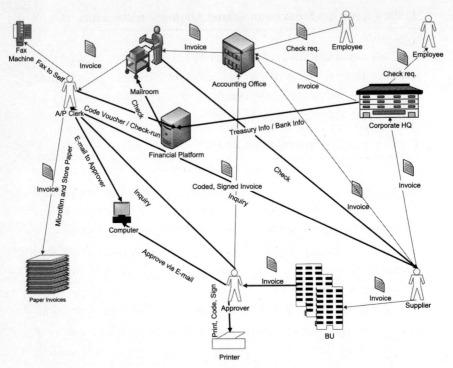

FIGURE 5.3 Manual A/P Invoice Processing

The first two drivers were enabled by implementing an invoice receipt and approval work flow automation solution. The third was achieved through the launch of a P-card program for small-dollar purchases. Using a P-card in this controlled fashion removed a large volume of small-value invoices from the A/P workload. Together, the three drivers changed the A/P metrics to the ones shown in Table 5.2.

The initiative to optimize the A/P invoice process was completed in 18 weeks, including a request for proposal for selecting the technology vendor as well as a vendor for outsourcing parts of the process and implementing the solution complete with a pilot of the new end-to-end process. The new optimized process is shown in Figure 5.4.

TABLE 5.2 Metrics for Semiautomated A/P Invoice Processing

Metric	Value
Invoices processed per month	20,000
FTE count for invoice processing	9
Invoices processed per FTE per year	26,666
Average days invoice ready for payment	6
Cost for invoice ready for payment	$5

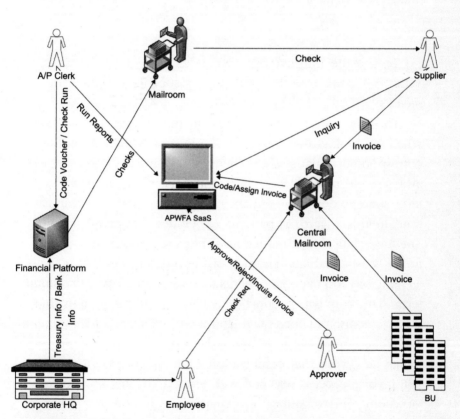

FIGURE 5.4 Semiautomated A/P Invoice Processing

TABLE 5.3 Pre- and Post-Process Optimization Metrics Comparison

Metric	Old Value	New Value	Improvement
FTE count for invoice processing	27	9	18 FTE freed up for other tasks
Invoices processed per FTE per year	9,777	26,666	72.3% productivity increase
Average days invoice ready for payment	42	6	85.7% cycle time improvement
Cost for invoice ready for payment	$15	$5	66.7% reduction in cost

To see the improvements made as part of this initiative, Table 5.3 compares the pre- and post-process optimization metrics.

The true value of this change in metrics can be realized when we look at the impact on the income statement and the corresponding balance sheet changes. Looking at these changes at a discrete point in time may not make obvious their long-term shareholder value-enhancing influence for the organization. In this regard, it pays to remember that these are not one-time tactical cost reductions. They are permanent changes in the "cost-capability" balance of the organization that generate tangible and material benefits that accumulate over the long term. The cumulative effect is realized in terms of a higher positive economic percentage and therefore shareholder value.

While impressive in terms of the working capital improvements achieved, this organization's journey of optimizing its A/P invoice process was not over. From a systems and process viewpoint, this organization managed to achieve the second stage of A/P optimization as depicted in Figure 5.5.

Reaching Stage 3 of A/P automation for this business would mean achieving end-to-end digitization of the procure-to-pay

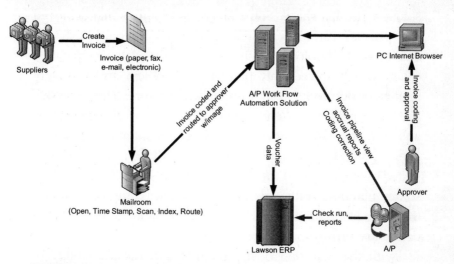

FIGURE 5.5 Stage 2 of A/P Automation

process resulting in straight-through processing (STP). Achieving this step would entail the key milestones of enabling:

- Electronic purchase order and invoice data exchange
- Electronic payments
- Electronic remittance advice
- Automatic approval of invoices

The benefit of this additional effort would be a further significant reduction in transaction costs with an equally meaningful increase in the velocity and transparency of critical working capital information.

Enabling Technologies

Not too many years ago, automating the transaction-intensive processes in A/P was difficult and expensive, primarily due to a lack of adequate and affordable information technology solutions in this space. Some large corporations that achieved A/P process automation, such as General Motors, used very expensive technology, such as electronic data interchange (EDI), which solved only part of the problem and was very inefficient due to its point-to-point architecture. The pervasive use of paper in the end-to-end P2P process hampered the ability to streamline processes to reduce manual touch points. Even as stand-alone applications such as Excel became "integrated" with high-end and costly platforms like enterprise resource planning (ERP), the process itself was still weak due to the many integration points that required manual input, causing data entry errors and delays.

With the maturing of the Internet and the availability of web-based enterprise applications, the time finally arrived for cost-effective, end-to-end integration of processes and subprocesses in the financial supply chain. Difficulties still remain due to a lack of universal public domain standards formats of the key documents involved in the P2P process including:

- Purchase order (PO)
- Invoice
- Goods receipt
- Remittance advice

Initial technology-enabled attempts, which we will call Stage 1 of A/P automation, were characterized by the emergence of applications that attempted to automate the transaction-oriented processes, such as invoice matching and payment reconciliation. These attempts were not very fruitful because they still relied on a paper document and required manual keying of data. The high rate of errors as well as the human-intensive nature of this approach provided limited benefits to the organization.

The second phase of A/P automation, Stage 2, uses imaging technology to convert paper documents into electronic images at either the back end of the process or the front end. Using scanners and optical character recognition, intelligent character recognition, and more recently intelligent capture software, P2P documents such as invoices can be converted into legally acceptable images of the original. As of late 2009, this is the most widely pursued approach to A/P automation. Although companies taking this approach are no doubt better off than those that are still in Stage 1, they nevertheless are missing the lion's share of the benefit to be derived from A/P process optimization and automation. The reason for this is that even with this process improvement, the paper document does not go away. It still exists within the financial supply chain, causing higher-than-necessary costs and longer-than-acceptable cycle times.

Stage 3 of A/P process automation has arrived, and it brings us close to the long-awaited milestone of eliminating paper from the P2P process. The key feature of this stage of solutions is the enablement of EIPP. With EIPP, the key documents involved in the P2P process—the purchase order and the invoice—are originated, exchanged, processed, and archived electronically. This drastically reduces the costs and cycle times for all trading partners involved in the transaction, end to end. When all key data are available in electronic format, these key benefits can finally be realized:

- Automated data validation at the point of receipt of invoice
- Automated business rules application for PO-invoice matching
- Automated rules-based routing and approval of non-PO invoices

- STP of PO invoices
- Real-time notification of invoice receipt and payment status to the appropriate party

The marketplace for products in this stage is still growing. Various technology solutions providers have taken a few different approaches to support Stage 3 of A/P automation; some are still offering Stage 2 solutions. The list shown in Table 5.4 is by no means exhaustive, but it does present some of the key players in each of the three major categories of solution providers.

Each of these approaches is briefly described next.

TABLE 5.4 Approaches Taken by A/P Automation Solution Providers

	Stand-alone Workflow Automation (WFA)	ERP and Add-on	Buyer-Supplier Network
170 Systems		X	
Accu-Image	X		
AnyDoc Software	X		
Archive Systems	X		
Ariba	X		X
BasWare	X		X
Brainware	X		
Concur	X		
DataBank IMX	X		
Digital Designs	X		
EMC	X		
Metafile Systems	X		X
OB10			X
Oracle		X	
ReadSoft		X	
SAP		X	
Symphony Services*	X		
Xign (JPMorgan)	X		X

*Symphony Services provides value-added services built around its work flow platform.

118

Stand-alone Applications

Stand-alone applications solve a niche category of problems. In this case, they solve the A/P automation problem in innovative ways. They are not hampered by the integration and compatibility issues faced by broader-scoped ERP platforms. They also enjoy the flexibility of being able to solve the problem by combining one or more of the approaches outlined earlier.

ERP Modules and ERP Add-ons

ERP platform providers have consistently expanded their solution offering by adding modules of functionality that were previously considered the domain of stand-alone applications. This encroachment on the turf of these specialized applications came with a downside; earlier modules that were competing with specialized applications were not as robust; they offered the most basic and common functionality. As ERP applications have matured, their vendors have been compelled to expand the scope of their platforms in order to grab and retain a larger portion of the market share. A/P is one of the areas where these platforms have expanded relatively recently. As was the case with their entry into other functions, such as treasury, their A/P automation offerings as a category of solution are not as robust as those from other categories. The biggest challenge is the cost and effort of tweaking the ERP platform to make it work with other components of the P2P process automation solution.

To address this shortcoming, a subcategory of solutions has become available consisting of add-ons to the ERP platform. This is not a new idea and has been a viable model for technology solution providers from both a technical and a business model perspective. The add-on solution provides highly focused specialized functionality while leveraging ERP's core financial features. From a solution purchaser's viewpoint, this is a desirable approach since it results in a familiar user interface, out-of-the-box integration, and a lower cost and time of implementation. It also leverages the customer's existing investment in the ERP platform.

Network Approach

From a business model perspective, the network approach is based on leveraging the combined transaction volume both from buyers and suppliers. The biggest benefits to both buyers and suppliers include:

- Lowest transaction costs of any other model
- Low cost of implementation
- Shortest time to implementation

Some of the leading solution providers in this category are:

- Ariba
- OB10
- Xign

The network approach is depicted in Figure 5.6.

For example, OB10 is a leading provider of a global network of e-invoicing. It provides a "many-to-many" invoice format mapping service that goes a long way toward increasing its value propositions to the widest possible number of suppliers and buyers. Previously, large companies used EDI over a Value-Added Network (VAN), EDI-VAN connectivity with larger supply chain partners. But EDI is a very expensive and invasive point-to-point solution. OB10's approach is to leverage the Internet for smaller suppliers with low invoice volumes while offering an "integrated" solution for higher-volume suppliers.

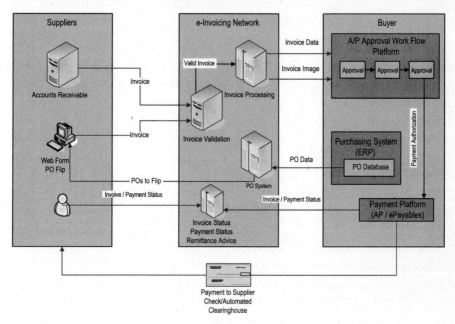

FIGURE 5.6 e-Invoicing Network

The flexibility of using their existing format to deliver invoices to the network is a huge benefit for all suppliers and removes the last hurdle from taking advantage of this capability.

Case Study

A large law firm with multiple offices nationwide in the United States and Europe launched a program to identify opportunities for profit maximization. One key area that quickly emerged as a candidate for optimization was accounts payable. Not only was the invoice processing being done based on paper invoices, but staff assigned to this task at each of the offices created a log-jam of invoices

(Continued)

121

at period-close and a lack of visibility into the payables liability from a cash management viewpoint.

The decision was made to leverage the opportunity for creating a shared services group within the financial back office and use A/P as the starting point. After mapping the processes and working out the many variations that existed because each office did things a little differently for no justifiable reason, a unified common process was designed that would support the specific needs of the legal business in a very effective and efficient manner. The next step was the automation of this process to move from a paper-intensive method to a digitized one. Using a structured approach for objective decision making, the team identified the key drivers for the projected value to be delivered by the initiative. This led to the selection of a technology solution provider that would best meet the needs of the organization.

The system went live in 24 weeks, including a pilot with a limited number of suppliers and a handful of offices. In the first year, the law firm was able to achieve these results:

- 85% reduction in cost of processing an invoice
- Ability to pay an invoice in 5 days versus 35 days
- Over 45% reduction in archival and internal audit costs
- Virtual elimination of lost and duplicate invoices

Conclusion

The accounts payable function historically has been a slow-moving, high-pressure, transaction-focused part of the financial back office, predominantly due to the extensive use of paper documents within the core A/P processes: purchase order, invoice, and goods receipt. More important is the fact that management in general has failed to see the strategic value of the A/P function. The A/P function has been considered a cost center from which cash of the organization flows out; the aim has been to keep the A/P function focused on transactional work, work harder and faster, and just hold on to that cash as long as possible.

Although the Internet has enabled cost-effective solutions to solve the fundamental problems behind this historic state of A/P, most organizations have been very slow to react to this opportunity. What is worse is that when they do become aware of the enormous opportunity for optimizing working capital through A/P process improvement and automation, a lot of these organizations get bogged down in the low-level details of the technology and fail to realize the benefits in a timely fashion. It would behoove these companies to hire outside experts to reduce the time to benefit realization instead of using in-house resources who have never implemented the process before and also have a day job to attend to. The most important thing to do in this regard is to do something, the sooner the better. Real value is at stake.

Note

1 Mary S. Schaeffer, *Accounts Payable Best Practices* (Hoboken, NJ: John Wiley & Sons, 2004); and Steven Bragg, *Accounting Best Practices* (Hoboken, NJ: John Wiley & Sons, 2005).

CHAPTER 6

Optimizing Accounts Receivable

Lack of money is the root of all evil.

—George Bernard Shaw

A company can literally sell itself right out of business if it does not have a strong accounts receivable (A/R) function. While this does not happen very often, a variation is common. Businesses of all sizes and types, and in almost all industries, leak revenue before it gets to the bottom line. The amount of leakage varies and is highly dependent on the business model and the efficiency and effectiveness of the entire Order-to-Cash process including the A/R function. Trade credit sales that cannot be collected according to terms, at their full value (less any agreed-on trade discounts) and within the time frame, lose value for the enterprise. As the volume of these value Losing sales increases, the firm's cash flow is adversely impacted, and the balance sheet gets loaded with receivables that are at risk of being written off. Once again, the organization has to achieve collaboration across all functional areas that generate revenues or support working capital in any way. This holistic approach is the only sustainable path to maximizing profitability. In this chapter, we explore the most important A/R processes and metrics that impact working capital and hence profitability.

Implications of A/R Effectiveness

Managing cash inflows from credit sales efficiently is critical for staying in business. The A/R function has the responsibility not only for collecting on credit sales but also for ensuring that the optimal credit policies are in place that maximize sales while minimizing bad debt write-offs. The efficiency and effectiveness of this function is crucial to the profitability of a corporation.

A/R is the primary gateway for the largest cash inflows for an organization. For vast majority of small and medium business (SMB) enterprises in the United States, 60% of working capital is tied up in A/R. It is also one of the three largest tangible assets for 75% of U.S. companies. Given these data, it is quite clear that managing this asset through highly efficient and effective processes should be a very high priority for any business organization that wants to grow and thrive. While management often understands how important this is, it does not always know how to go about achieving this efficiency. Some organizations believe that utilizing the newest technology solutions would do the job in this area; others believe that outsourcing the function to a third party would achieve the objective. Both of these approaches can be a component of a sound strategy, but seldom has either been a success strategy in itself. Automating or outsourcing a poorly designed process will only lead to more problems and waste of valuable time and resources. The results achieved by many firms that tried to streamline the process in-house have been disappointing. This should be no surprise, when in-house staff members who are not experienced in process optimization and not thoroughly familiar with the various automation technology options and their pros and cons are asked to tackle this challenge. Enterprise value is enhanced when a capable team with vast experience in this area is engage to analyze, plan, and execute the optimization initiative. When a firm is operating at a suboptimal level, each day of delay in optimizing the process results is lost enterprise value.

As we have discussed earlier in this book, there is no shortcut to sustainable profitability. It is achieved through a well-designed strategy that is enabled by a platform for execution that is fully aligned with that strategy. A/R is no exception. The first task is to develop a strategy for optimizing this function. What processes does the organization desire to build a core competency in? Where do its strengths lie in this regard? What are the risk factors that it must consider, and what are their implications? A careful analysis would lead to answers to these sorts of questions:

- Should we use an outside collection agency?
- Should we outsource billing?
- Does it make sense to develop our own credit scoring model?
- What kind of customer segmentation should we use to manage portfolio risk?

Having analyzed these factors, the strategy should start to emerge. This strategy should be in alignment with corporate risk and return objectives, as these will have an impact on its growth.

The next step is to map the strategy components to specific back-office business processes, in this case, A/R processes. This is a key step and must not be taken lightly or skipped. The mapping of strategy components to business processes generally is not done or is conducted in a very unscientific manner producing less-than-optimal results. The advice here is to use Lean methodology and tools for this purpose, in order to make objective decisions. Specifically, a tool such as a critical–to–return on investment (ROI) (CTR) analysis grid is very well suited for this purpose. An example of a CTR analysis for mapping strategy components to A/R processes is shown in Figure 6.1.

In the left column are listed the objectives we want to achieve but do not have direct control over. These are the critical factors for success. Across the top row to the right of the CTR Ranking column are listed the influencing factors. These are the things we can control in order to achieve our objectives. The second column from the left contains a ranking of the CTR factors in terms of their importance, with one being the least important and five being the most important. Note that it contains odd values only because we cannot have more than two factors with the same ranking in order for this model to work effectively. People first using this tool tend to make everything most important. It pays to remember that this is an exercise in objectivity. We must force ourselves to makes choices regarding what is most important. In the grid below the influencing factors and to the right of the CTR ranking column is a ranking of each influencing factor against each CTR factor. This ranking is designed to gauge how strongly we believe the influencing factor affects the CTR factor. The ranking goes from zero, meaning no influence on the CTR factor, to nine, meaning strong influence, and again contains only odd values. The result of this model is a coverage map of all the influencing factors for all the CTR factors. The tools provide an objective rank order of the driver of ROI, based on the collective input of the participants in the analysis. The rankings may change, but only as a result of the team's collective input. In this example, the top three drivers of ROI are:

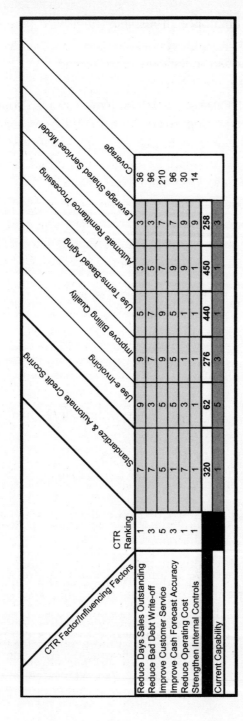

FIGURE 6.1 CTR Analysis for Objective Decision Making

1. Automate remittance processing

2. Use terms-based aging

3. Standardize and automate credit scoring

With this analysis in hand, the team can go about creating a road map for putting these drivers of ROI into action. This exact tool has been used in many initiatives with great success.

Best Practices

From a process and technology perspective, the best practices for A/R include:

- Automation of deductions processing
- Automation of creation of late payment fees and unearned prompt payment discounts
- Customer segmentation for portfolio risk management
- Credit scoring model that includes hard and soft parameters
- Automated credit sale authorization with hard and soft controls
- Terms-based aging of receivables
- Automation of routine collection activities (e.g., dunning letters)
- Customer relationship–focused collections activities
- Frequent process benchmarking

In order to achieve a truly world class A/R operation, an organization first must discard its traditional way of thinking about the financial back-office functions as silos. Historically, these silos have existed primarily due to a lack of automation technology that could integrate information. This constraint led to the development of processes that were anything but efficient. In the absence of cost-effective automation alternatives, businesses relied on humans to execute the process tasks and to integrate information manually. The cycle times and errors in the manual processes were very high, ultimately resulting is equally high costs in the financial back-office functions, including A/R.

Today we have a wide array of Web-based automation technology solutions available for the various processes in the back office. The problem now is not of a lack of automation options but an overwhelming number and variety of them. An organization whose core competency is not selecting and implementing these solutions is at a great disadvantage when it attempts to execute the myriad tasks involved in such an endeavor. The staff that is trained in and is good at operational tasks is generally not adept at managing change including selecting and deploying state of the art solutions. It is best to engage an outside neutral party (not a technology vendor itself) that specializes in this work and has extensive prior experience in this area. The focus should remain on ROI, not on price. As we have discussed before, it is not in the best interest of the organization to get a low upfront price in return for a greater long term cost, be it in the form of total cost of ownership (TCO) or the opportunity cost arising from a less than optimal process.

Create a Road Map for Optimization

Optimizing the A/R function entails developing a carefully designed road map that is in alignment with the objectives of the organization and takes into consideration the specifics of its industry, business environment, and culture. No one-size-fits-all strategy can deliver success in this context. Taking small steps and gaining early victories help build morale and add to the momentum for optimization efforts. In addition, not all efforts yield equal value. Keeping these two points in mind, the best practice approach for building the road map would proceed in this way:

- Benchmark the key performance indicators
- Assess the state of technology capability
- Analyze areas of greatest financial benefit (cash application, late fees, and discount management, bad debt write-offs)
- Evaluate the state of the art for automation
- Build an architecture that aligns with the overall financial back-office platform for execution
- Establish realistic milestones and timelines for optimization

This list hides the complexities involved in its execution. This inherent complexity of the tasks involved is one of the primary reasons why most organizations, even after they realize the sustainable benefits to be achieved by optimizing their financial back-office processes, are unwilling or unable to embark on this journey. This lack of action is a direct result of a lack of experience, expertise, and resources. Those organizations that have taken the bold step in this direction have found that the benefits far outweigh the costs, perceived or real.

Prioritize Attention to Distressed and Delinquent Accounts

Like sales, collection of delinquent accounts requires constant attention. Companies that consistently maximize profitability are proactive in contacting customers whose accounts are at risk of becoming delinquent. By tracking the patterns of payments and aging of accounts to gauge the financial conditions of their customers, they can detect a problem before it is too late. One of the major signs of distress on the customer's financial situation is late payment of bills. Other signs include cash shortages, degrading gross profit margins, frequent operating losses, inconsistent financial reporting schedules, or a general lack of information.

A common trend among companies is to contact a consumer customer a few days after a missed payment date. Some organizations send a reminder letter or make a call a few days before payment is due. This contact may originate from A/R, customer service, or sales and also can be used to confirm receipt of goods and to verify that invoice and shipping documents were in order. No matter what form this contact takes, its purpose is to remove any potential barriers to receiving a payment.

Accounts that do become delinquent should be classified by risk. Each risk group has a specific plan of action assigned to it. Collection staff should be given support through process automation to eliminate repetitive tasks as well as latitude in working with customers to determine the most realistic payment solution for each incident. The first step here is to evaluate the delinquent customer's situation and determine exactly why the payment has not been made and the likelihood that payment will be made in the near future. Paramount in this context is the effort to avoid alienating potential long-term customers. Some of the best practices being used for this purpose include:

- Customer-specific collections policies
- Flexibility with options, such as renegotiating sales contracts or payment terms
- Requiring cash for future orders
- Initiating stop-shipment
- Putting a hold on service policies
- Refusing to take additional orders until accounts are paid in full

Refocus Resources on High-Value Transactions

Some of the areas where A/R staff typically expend considerable amounts of time include:

- Deductions management
- Cash application
- Late fees and unearned early-payment discounts management

In each of these areas, the fundamental reason why this time is spent is misalignment of information between buyer and seller. There is no value created for the business enterprise in these areas no matter how efficiently the work is done. The obvious solution here is to not have to do this. Most companies, however, are not willing or able to avoid these areas, particularly cash application, which must be done. A better solution is to minimize the amount of work done in these areas.

In order to minimize the number of transactions that actually are handled in these areas, several steps have to be taken. Each of these steps can and should be supported by the appropriate set of information technology solutions:

- Move to e-Invoicing to minimize data entry errors.
- Use automated purchase order (PO) flip (generating an invoice directly from a PO) to reduce PO-invoice mismatches.
- Negotiate deductions thresholds with buyers, and execute these automatically
- Categorize and prioritize late fees and unearned early-payment discount transactions for exception handling.

The idea is to focus precious resources on a lower volume of transactions that would create incremental value for the company and not handle every transaction, no matter how little impact it has on the bottom line.

Monetize Accounts Receivable

The value of working capital for companies is well known to financial executives and business owners. Greater financial flexibility and the opportunity for growth are the reward for efficiently managing working capital. For SMBs, however, the greatest portion of their working capital is tied up in A/R. This is a result of trade credit practices whereby a seller extends payment terms to its customers to allow them to buy goods and services on account. The customers do not have to pay cash immediately, thus creating accounts receivable for the seller and accounts payable for the buyer. According to one estimate, over $1 trillion is tied up in trade credit in the United States alone. The average receivables turnover is 44 days, meaning that it takes 44 days for the seller to collect payment from the buyer. This is a strain on the working capital for SMBs. The extension of trade credit is essentially a free loan to the buyer and must be managed carefully. Since the buyer wants to use this free loan for as long possible and the seller wants to collect on this loan as soon as possible, there naturally results a tug-of-war between the business-to-business trading partners. This is evident in the desire of financial managers in the buying organizations to extend their days payables outstanding as far out as possible. On the flip side, for the seller, positive working capital must be financed. This cost of capital borrowed to fund the working capital gap results in reduced margins for the seller. Holding 44 days of A/R balance without a return has an opportunity cost for the seller, as measured by its lost return on equity (ROE). This cost results from not being able to collect the cash for the sale immediately and reinvest it in the business to earn the marginal ROE.

Using the cash conversion cycle (CCC) as the indicator of the efficiency with which a business converts its cash back into cash through its operating cycle, we can see that shorter the CCC, higher the ROE for a company. This higher ROE is directly linked to the enterprise value-added concept discussed in Chapter 1.

One way to speed up the CCC is to sell the receivables. Traditionally, this has involved the use of third parties that provide factoring services. These services are available at a very high cost; the average factoring discount rates are well above 12% and even as high as 40%. Due to their limited access to other sources of lower cost funding, a lot of SMBs are forced to take this option. However, lately, a new way to receivables monetizing has emerged that is gaining ground rapidly, fueled by the appetite of Wall Street firms to maximize their return on any asset they can invest in for a given risk level. The risk inherent in a company's receivables can be analyzed and measured using historical data. Therefore, this receivables asset constitutes viable investment with its own risk profile, using the principles of asset-based lending. As long as there is a market for buyers and sellers of receivables to conduct transactions, a company can sell its receivables to shorten its CCC and reinvest the cash in generating more revenue.

Such a marketplace for exchanging receivables does in fact exist in the form of the Receivables Exchange (www. ReceivablesXchange.com). This online marketplace combines the ability to transfer investment data electronically with the ability to make electronic transactions on those investments. On this exchange, a company can offer its receivables for sale to interested buyers and reduce its CCC as well as cost of capital.

The execution of this concept within the context of the financial supply chain is depicted in Figure 6.2.

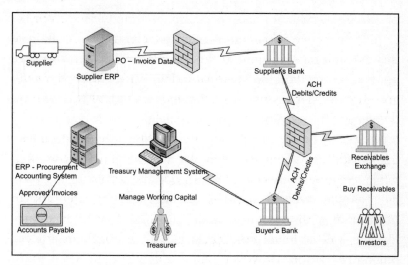

FIGURE 6.2 Receivables Exchange in a Financial Supply Chain

Enabling Technologies

The marketplace that caters to the financial back-office needs of corporations is buzzing with excitement regarding working capital optimization. A strong evidence of this lies in the fact that two acronyms have gained broad popularity and following; WCO and SCF, both of which have been discussed in Chapter 3 of this book. WCO stands for working capital optimization and SCF stands for supply chain finance. What we want to explore now is how these two key concepts integrate with what procurement considers its key objectives and what technologies exist to enable this integration.

In the context of financial supply chain, it is no longer in the best interest of buying organizations to think in terms of a zero-sum game when it comes to interacting and doing business with supply chain participants. Leading companies are using win-win approaches to optimizing and strengthening their supply chains. One of the key risks to any supply chain is the failure of its weakest link. If a supplier goes out

137

of business, whether unexpectedly or otherwise, a definite ripple effect goes through the buying organizations. To mitigate this risk, information sharing is needed as well as collaborative approaches to working capital funding needs for both buyer and supplier. This is where SCF comes into play. The concept is simple: The payables liability obligation of a creditworthy buyer can be sold to a third-party investor in order to create immediate cash flow for the entity to which the liability is owed while creating a desirable return for the investor. To look at it another way, a supplier can sell its receivables to an investor at a discount for immediate cash needs. It sounds like the long-standing practice of factoring, but there is a big difference.

Without getting into the details of factoring, such as with recourse or without, we will mention two critical deficiencies with it, as they affect the original owner of the receivables being factored. The first one has to do with the discount rate. Factoring is a terrible choice for a company looking for liquidity and cash flow as it entails discount rates that can run from 1% to 5% of the A/R value and in some cases as high as 10%!. In most of the cases, this rate ranges from 3% to 5%. For a receivable that the factor accepts, it typically gives 85% of the invoice value to the client immediately. The rest of the amount, minus the discount, will be given upon payment of the invoice. As we can see, this may take a while if the buyer delays paying the invoice. So, the first problem with factoring is that it comes at a high cost and even then does not deliver the maximum cash flow possible immediately. The second problem with factoring is more strategic in nature. It has to do with customer relationship management. A factor, depending on the terms of the agreement with the client and the services it has agreed to provide, may take proactive steps to collect on the invoices it has factored. As we saw in the example of Dell in Chapter 2, outside entities should not be given control over functions of a business that relate to customer service. A factor may well jeopardize the business relationship between a buyer and a supplier by using aggressive collections techniques. After all, the factor's discount fees are tied to the collection of the invoice. This concern is compounded by the fact that factoring typically is used for invoices of large dollar amounts, which means they are for the entity's more valuable customers.

A better approach for solving the cash-crunch problem for the receivables owner is the use of newly emerging platforms and financial services that are the domain of SCF. One of the enablers of SCF transactions is a company called PrimeRevenue. PrimeRevenue brings buyers, suppliers, and financial institutions across the globe together through its technology platform. Its services enable these trading partners to exchange "value" as it may suit their specific situation. For example, let's say a supplier has a $1 million invoice that has been approved by the buyer and that the payment terms are 45 days. If the supplier needs faster access to cash from this invoice, it can use the PrimeRevenue platform to offer its receivable for sale to an interested third-party investor (a financial institution) at a discount. The financial institution would offer a discount rate based on the creditworthiness of the buyer, which is available within the PrimeRevenue platform immediately. Without any undue delay, the transaction can be executed. Settlement of the full amount of the invoice, less the discount, takes place on the next business day. For the supplier, the high speed and low cost of the transaction are tremendous improvements over the factoring route. The financial institution has the opportunity to earn a good return on a short-term investment that is in line with the risk-return components of its investment portfolio. The buyer benefits by getting the ability to extend the payment according to terms without jeopardizing the supply chain through financial risk to the supplier.

Ariba (www.ariba.com)

Getting invoices paid promptly can be a challenge for most organizations in the SME category. Yet at the same time, it is these businesses that are at the greatest risk from delinquent payments impacting cash flow. This situation exists primarily due to the use of paper documents in the procure-to-pay process. Incorrect formatting, missing information, inaccurate contact data, and many other issues can cause accounts payable to block payment on an invoice that may take days or weeks to resolve. In addition, the A/R function in the seller organization may not know anything is wrong until an invoice is past due, further delaying compensation.

Seller organization can greatly alleviate this problem by eliminating paper from the process. Using Ariba's Supplier Network, for example, a seller can manage the complete life cycle of its invoice electronically, making it accurate, efficient, and less costly. The combined benefit is that the seller gets paid faster. The network offers many options to suit the needs of sellers and buyers including:

- Purchase order flip
- CSV upload
- cXML interface
- Electronic Data Interchange (EDI)

When using any of these options, it is very important to meet the buyer's billing requirements, such as:

- Valid PO number or buyers information (for non-PO invoices)
- Correct quantity
- Correct unit of measure
- Accurate line item and details

- Accurate invoice total
- Correct terms
- Separate shipping charges
- Proper handling of sales and use tax

The network assists sellers by validating buyer-specific data at the time of invoice submission and by providing the seller with instant notification of invoice acceptance or rejection. The rejecting of invoices at the front end that eventually would be not paid by the buyer alone saves ample time .

The Ariba Supplier Network also offers a feature called dynamic discounting, which allows the seller to offer its customers automated discounts when they elect to pay their invoices early. The seller enjoys greater control over its invoicing policy and is better able to manage the receivables component of its working capital. Additional benefits result in the form of reduced days sales outstanding (DSO) and on-time payment since the buyers are given an incentive to pay invoices sooner. It also reduces or eliminates one of the most time-consuming transactions in A/R that adds little value: deductions processing.

OB10

OB10 operates a global network that enables e-Invoicing. Its solutions are developed with the recognition that there is a direct correlation between paper invoice processing and payment uncertainty. This results in inefficient working capital management due to excess cash being tied up in the order-to-cash cycle to form a hedge against the payment uncertainty.

The OB10 model is built around supplier enablement. Its value proposition to the buyers includes:

- Eliminating paper from the process
- Reducing invoice receipt time from days to minutes

- Detecting and acting on invoice errors at the front end
- Using electronic invoice data to enable intelligent routing and work flow
- Immediate supplier access to invoice receipt and payment status

The sum total of these benefits is a reduction in process cost for invoices and supplier inquiries for payment status. The reduction in cycle times leads to the ability to negotiate better payment terms, through either early-pay discounts or more favorable prices.

OB10 allows sellers to choose the way they want to send invoices. It provides flexible submission options that accommodate a seller's transaction volume and invoice format and structure. Since no changes to the seller's existing billing systems and procedures are required, it is very easy for the sellers to join the network and reap immediate and lasting benefits.

Basware

Basware (www.basware.com) provides end-to-end automation of the purchase-to-pay process using its technology platform and outsourced services model. It enables both buyer and supplier organizations to leverage its technology and services to achieve eA/P-2 level of capabilities in their financial supply chain.

Basware Business Transactions is a monitored transfer and conversion service for e-invoices and other purchasing-related documents, such as e-orders. It converts e-invoices and other purchasing-related documents into the correct format and delivers them to the right recipients through one single connection to suppliers and buyers.

Basware Supplier Portal is a web interface for suppliers to key in invoices, receive orders electronically, send order confirmations, and upload and create electronic catalogs. The buyer is able to use the same Business Transactions platform to integrate to its invoice processing and procurement solutions.

Basware Scan and Capture is a fully outsourced service to convert all paper invoices to electronic format. Basware provides the scanning and validation of incoming paper invoices and delivers them to the buyer's invoice processing system. Coupled with the Basware Supplier Activation service, converting from paper invoices to true e-invoices enables a firm to reduce processing costs even further.

Basware Supplier Activation is an outsourced service to communicate with suppliers and assist them to connect to the buyers' purchase-to-pay process.

Case Study

Driven by a pressing need to pay down its debt, a $3 billion organization in the commercial chemicals industry needed better visibility into its cash inflows and outflows. It took a top-down approach to making its customer-to-cash process transparent and to speed up the flow of information as well as cash throughout the organization, leading to much more accurate cash forecasting. This capability would enable treasury to make better decisions about short-term borrowing and investing.

The project team looked at the entire end-to-end process and streamlined it using best practices and automation. It was designed for the complexities of the distribution network where collections were taking place as well as for the seasonality of A/R balances in its portfolio.

(Continued)

143

The team gathered requirements from treasury and the rest of finance for information and metrics in order to create a process that would optimize both while also reducing the operational costs. The results listed DSO and average days delinquent as the top metrics. Information requirements also pointed out a need to use customer segmentation to optimize revenue risk within the credit and collections process. The process for capturing and recording information on customers' promise to pay was redesigned to make it systematic and was linked to the handling of aged receivables.

The streamlined processes were automated using an automation solution for cash management. This system enabled configuration of business rules that would automate the routine tasks in the collections process. The A/R team was then able to focus on the activities of monitoring and managing cash collections and forecasting.

The end result of this effort to improve the efficiency of the A/R processes was a drop in the average past-due balance by over $25 million as compared to the previous year and a decrease in average deductions balance of over $2 million. The DSO was reduced by four days as a result, and the improved cash flow and cash forecasting accuracy have added an estimated $2.5 million to the bottom line. Treasury now has far better visibility into the cash flow pipeline to make better cash management decisions.

Conclusion

Accounts receivable processes play a critical role in the effective management of working capital. Not only is the information within its processes vital to the cash management and liquidity needs of the organization, these same processes also are the main conduit of the firm's cash inflows. The sheer volume of transactions in A/R makes a strong case for process optimization, automation, integration, and standardization, all leading to significant efficiencies.

Optimizing and automating A/R processes delivers benefits in terms of improving the quality of customer experience, process output, employee morale and productivity, and overall financial performance of the organization. However, in order to achieve these results, the approach taken must be based on scientific methods. In this regard, the tools and methods of lean six sigma are invaluable in the hands of a team that has done this work in the same context before. Using fundamental process improvement and then automation can open opportunities for further optimization by leveraging a shared services model. This is the path increasingly being taken by leading organizations.

CHAPTER 7

Optimizing Purchasing

A study of economics usually reveals that the best time to buy anything is last year.

—Marty Allen

Purchasing, or procurement, as it is increasingly being referred to, is responsible for sourcing raw materials and goods, for both operating and capital needs. Generally speaking, the term "purchasing" is understood to represent the transactional and administrative aspects of the function while "procurement" represents the strategic ones. For the purpose of this book, we will use the terms interchangeably.

Purchasing is one of the biggest areas of corporate spend, aside from payroll, and therefore it is focused on spend management. The liabilities created through purchasing activities have a direct and significant impact on the corporation's financial performance. To further enhance the value of this function, collaboration among supply chain, procurement, and finance can create a true competitive advantage for an organization through lower cost of goods sold, lower operating expenses, and therefore higher operating margins and profitability. One of the key advantages of such collaboration is the increased cash velocity and transparency of information. Combined, these two factors have a more positive impact on working capital than anything else that is within the organization's control. This advantage adds directly to the economic value of a business in good economic times. In adverse economic times, it takes on an even more important role that can mean the difference between survival and bankruptcy. In this chapter, we explore what specifically can be done within the procurement function.

The performance of a business enterprise as it relates to procurement can be measured by four metrics:

1. Cost of direct and indirect materials and services
2. Customer service
3. Cash conversion cycle
4. Demand forecast accuracy

Optimization performance on the basis of these metrics leads to a differentiation between industry leaders and the rest. Optimization is truly a complex balancing act. As an example, it would not be in the best interest of the organization if procurement acquired vast quantities of raw materials at a great price for which there was no immediate or foreseeable demand. While it may look like a good move from the perspective of reducing direct materials costs in the short term, it actually may hurt the business enterprise's due to cash being tied up in working capital for an unnecessarily long period. It may also result in stock obsolescence if the raw materials are turned into work in progress or finished goods inventory without the demand to secure a sale. Keeping a close eye on the cash conversion cycle (CCC) metric would enable the procurement function not to lose sight of the forest for the trees. One of the ways in which the procurement function can avoid such a situation is to focus heavily on improving demand forecasting accuracy. This is a collaborative task. Sales, marketing, finance, production, and customer service areas of the organization must work closely with procurement to achieve the desired performance at the business-wide level.

Implications of Purchasing Effectiveness

The world is changing rapidly, and this means that business practices in the procurement function have to evolve to keep pace. What used to be best business practices as recently as five years ago are no longer in the best interest of the organization. Senior management that neglects to pay attention to this reality puts the organization at great risk and loses vital competitive edge as a result. A short case study will illustrate the point. The events are real and related to the very recent past: the global economic downturn that began in 2007.

A large manufacturing business had a strong procurement function. It had policies and procedures in place to ensure that it continuously monitored the strength of its supply chain, end to end, and took appropriate steps to address any weak links that were found on occasion. It had carefully forged strategic supplier relationships for souring materials at very competitive prices. This effort in procurement showed in the financial results and the key performance metrics, such as CCC and gross margin.

As the economy softened, the finance function initiated steps to protect liquidity by slowing down cash outflows, primarily by lengthening its days payables outstanding. This

(Continued)

conservative approach was an appropriate method that has been the standard tactical tool of finance for a long time. As we have discussed before, the buyer's payables are the supplier's receivables. One of the sole-source suppliers of a critical material was severely impacted by the global economic downturn and the ensuing credit crunch. Unable to raise sufficient short-term funding for its working capital needs, this supplier was forced to go out of business without any warning to the buyer; the manufacturing company. The material it provided was critical to the main product, and the manufacturer was in the middle of fulfilling a large project. It took the manufacturer a couple of months to identify, qualify, and onboard an alternate supplier and to get the project moving forward again. Due to the cost of short-term funding it needed to cover the gap in its cash flow caused by interruption to forecasted cash inflows, the manufacturer's bottom line took a hit. Fortunately, the customer understood the causes of the delay in project delivery and was sympathetic to the manufacturer due to a long-standing relationship between the two organizations. Although this story ends on a relatively happy note, not all do.

A valuable lesson can be learned from this story. If the manufacturer had been aware of the financial situation of one of its key suppliers in a timely manner, it could have taken steps to prevent the situation from getting out of control. One of these steps could have been using its own stronger credit rating to secure funding for the supplier through supply chain finance (SCF). Another could have been ensuring that the payables for this supplier were not pushed out. The key idea here is that procurement and finance need to work together, providing information and guidance to each other to keep the organization performing at optimal efficiency. This synchronization is not an option; it is a requirement for maximizing profitability. Enabling this synchronization takes a carefully planned strategy, a platform for execution, and an organizational culture that is conducive to collaboration and information sharing across functional boundaries.

The reality is that this story is not unique. As the global economy continues to weaken, scenarios such as this one appear across the business landscape for buyers and suppliers alike. Suppliers in particular are vulnerable. Most that have gone out of business recently did so not because their business model was weak; rather, their cash flow dried up with no access to capital for funding their working capital. The failure of a supplier business weakens the supply chain and affects all participants in it, both upstream and downstream. In the end-to-end procure-to-pay circle, all players are dependent on the good health of all other players in the supply chain.

We can see the signs of this phenomenon in the current trend of increasingly more late business-to-business payments. It cannot be emphasized enough that extending payables, while it seems easy to do and beneficial to the organization doing it, is a tactic, not a strategy. The cost associated with it may be greater in the larger context than its benefit in the narrower context.

For procurement, it is no longer sufficient just to manage the corporate spend on direct and indirect materials. The strategic objective of procurement is to manage, minimize, and mitigate the supply chain risk. It also needs to work closely with finance, particularly accounts payable and treasury functions, to help the organization achieve maximum profitability. Leading business organizations are aware of this change in the role of procurement and understand the broader issue of financial chain risk. They also understand the range of strategies available to safeguard corporate earnings and profitability. Some of these strategies entail leveraging SCF for the benefit of the suppliers or even financing critical suppliers. This is not business as it used to be. The name of the game in today's fiercely competitive, rapidly changing, and fast-paced global business environment is collaboration, both within and outside the walls of a business enterprise.

When a procurement function utilizes best practices and has a broad and strategic vision in addition to transactional excellence, the organization can achieve its goals in working capital optimization, supply chain risk management, and total cost of ownership management for its direct and indirect spend. Given the finance function's focus on cash management, procurement can play a key role in helping finance by collaboratively managing the cash flows through sourcing activities and terms with suppliers.

Best Practices

The best practices in the procurement area are strategic in nature. Procedural best practices are well documented in other texts and are not the focus of this book. Some of the works that cover the procedural aspects of procurement and supply chain management include *Purchase Order Management Best Practices* and *Supply Chain Management*.[1] Procurement best practices at the strategic level include:

- Align closely with the objectives of the finance function.
- Create processes that increase the visibility of enterprise-wide spend as early as possible.
- Manage the supply chain risk diligently, including monitoring the financial health of key suppliers.

- Remember that price is not the most important factor in procurement; think of the total cost of ownership.
- Evaluate the structure, policies, and processes in terms of the key objective of enterprise profitability, not just profits.
- Provide and use accurate data necessary for making optimal procurement decisions.

In order to take advantage of these best practices, some fundamental capabilities are needed. As we saw in Chapter 4, a platform for execution is critical to the financial strength of a business enterprise. Procurement is a key user and contributor of the critical information that flows through this platform for the benefit of the entire organization. One of the key measures of profitability that procurement influences is days inventory outstanding (DIO). DIO is measured as:

$$DIO = (Average\ Inventory/Cost\ of\ Goods\ Sold) \times$$
$$Days\ in\ period$$

DIO measures the number of days that inventory stays in the system. The numerator is the average inventory calculated as the inventory at the beginning of the calculation period, plus the ending inventory, divided by 2, although just the ending inventory can be used as well. The denominator is the cost of goods sold (COGS) per day, which is a measure of how much inventory actually is used in each day of sales. This metric is a key component of another metric, inventory turns, used to determine the efficiency of inventory usage by a company. Inventory turns is measured as:

$$Inventory\ Turns = 360/DIO$$

Inventory turns measures how many times a year (if that is the measurement period) the entire inventory stock was sold and had to be replenished. It reflects how fast the cash invested in the inventory asset is turning back into cash and is one of

TABLE 7.1 Retail Industry Performance 2008

	Inventory Turns	Price/Earnings Ratio	Return on Equity	Return on Assets
Industry	8.5	15	19.5	7.7
Wal-Mart	8.7	14.4	21.1	8.3
Target	6.6	14.1	15	4.9

the key measures of management efficiency and effectiveness in creating economic value for the business enterprise. In the retail business, for example, a difference in inventory turns can mean success or failure. As an example, the 2008 performance data for two competitors in the retail industry is shown Table 7.1.

In this table, we see the comparative performance of two companies in the retail sector, both very large and successful operators. Target has an inventory turnover ratio of 6.6, which lags behind the industry average of 8.5. Wal-Mart's inventory turnover ratio of 8.7 leads the industry average. Now if we look at the profitability measure for these two companies, we see that, Target has a return on equity (ROE) of 15.0, which lags the industry average of 19.5. Wal-Mart has a ROE of 21.1, which leads the industry average. On another profitability measure, return on assets (ROA), Target has an industry-lagging 4.9 compared to the industry average of 7.7. Wal-Mart once again beats the industry average with an 8.3. All of this is accounted for in the valuations for these business enterprises by Wall Street, as reflected in their current price to earnings (P/E) ratios. The P/E for Target is 14.1, which lags Wal-Mart's 14.4. And although both lag the industry average P/E of 15, that in itself is not a bad sign. What matters here is how these two firms are valued against each other. As we can see clearly from this example, the procurement function has a definite impact not only on the bottom line of a business enterprise but also on its ultimate criterion of success: creating shareholder value as measured by economic profit and, in the case of a public firm, reflected in its market valuation. This impact of procurement is due to the fact that inventory is an asset and as such is created through the use of capital. For any business, the efficiency of capital use and the magnitude and quality of the returns on the investment of the capital determine the ultimate measure of success.

When we look at the DIO equation, the tactical aspects of procurement become obvious in the context of optimizing working capital. In order to minimize DIO—the desired goal—procurement can do one of two things, or both. It can reduce the numerator, the average inventory levels for a given period of measurement, or it can increase the denominator, its sales per day as measured by COGS per day. Since procurement does not have direct control over the denominator, it makes sense for this function to be deeply concerned with the numerator. This management of average inventory, as we saw earlier, is key to maximizing profitability.

How does procurement go about decreasing the average inventory? Some key considerations include:

- Volume purchase discounts
- Storage costs
- Transportation costs
- Lead time
- Stock outs
- Customer service

Addressing these considerations and balancing the forces that bear on the procurement function in its quest for creating enterprise value has been the concern of inventory management for a long time. A scientific method of optimizing inventory levels is called economic order quantity (EOQ). The equation for EOQ is:

$$EOQ = \sqrt{\frac{2(\text{Annual usage in units})(\text{Order cost})}{(\text{Annual carrying cost per unit})}}$$

EOQ is a mathematical formula that determines the point at which order costs and inventory carrying costs are minimized. This results in the most cost-effective quantity to order. In purchasing, this is known as the order quantity; in manufacturing, it is called the production lot size. The knowledge and indeed the use of this scientific approach to inventory management have been around since close to the beginning of the twentieth century. However, the results achieved by organizations in this regard have not been consistently good. A big part of this inconsistency in results lies in inaccurate data being input into the calculation of EOQ. We are not going to discuss the EOQ equation in detail here. The point that needs to be stressed is that this equation depends on the accuracy of its inputs. Most organizations do not have the accurate input data that is needed to make good use of this scientific method. Accurate product costs, activity costs, forecasts, history, and lead times are crucial in making inventory models work. The very fact that most enterprise resource planning (ERP) systems used by organizations concerned about managing inventory incorporate automatic EOQ calculations has led to users' lack of knowledge about how to use the tools properly. The users do not understand how EOQ is calculated and how the data inputs and system configuration affect the output. When system output does not align with expected results, it is simply ignored. In such situations, executives who authorized the purchase of the ERP software may incorrectly assume that the material planners and purchasing clerks are ordering based on the systems' recommendations. A key concern of procurement should be to promote the value of accurate data that is necessary for making sounds decisions

156

throughout the organization by collaborating with the other functions. This point cannot be overemphasized.

Let's face it: Sometimes the goals and strategies of a business enterprise may conflict with EOQ for various valid reasons, including the specifics of the organization's procurement needs. Performance in procurement cannot be measured by inventory turns alone. Thinking that inventory turns is the only key measure of performance for procurement is a common mistake made by many organizations. After achieving very impressive inventory management goals, these organizations find that their bottom line has shrunk due to increased operational costs. Once again, we need to remember that procurement is a very complex balancing act that involves dealing with objectives that are corporate wide and demanding collaboration among procurement and various other functions. At times, procurement objectives of securing certain payment terms from suppliers may not be aligned with overall corporate objectives.

As an example, procurement typically wants to negotiate terms that include early-pay discounts. Indeed, in most companies, successfully negotiating such discounts for the benefit of the enterprise is one of the measures of procurement function effectiveness. However, this effort may not always bear fruit as the cash flow implications of taking the discounts fluctuate with the seasonality of the business or other economic concerns. Best-in-class companies have taken a path that includes forming strategic relationships with vendors who can deliver on multiple levels, including vendor-managed inventory (VMI). VMI is a natural extension of the well-established concepts promoted and practiced in just-in-time (JIT) inventory management. As opposed to the JIT approach, where the buyer takes responsibility for managing its inventory levels, VMI transfers this task to the supplier. The buyer assists the supplier in delivering this critical capability by openly sharing its production and sales forecasts with the supplier. Doing this

157

entails a much closer buyer-supplier relationship than any other form of corporation-to-corporation relationship in the supply chain. The results of such close collaboration are impressive. Wal-Mart is a good example of using this approach to inventory management and procurement excellence.

Another key area in which procurement can help the organization gain a cost advantage is taxes. Although taxes are not a key concern of the procurement function in general, the area represents a ripe opportunity for contributing to maximizing profitability. In the global market of suppliers, where tax rates vary greatly among countries, all else being equal, buying from a supplier in a low-tax country versus a high-tax one can offer a buying organization a distinct advantage. The purchasing function can align with the internal tax department to ensure that the procurement strategy supports the tax optimization strategy. Once again, procurement is positioned to enhance the enterprise value through increased profitability.

Accurate determination of safety stock targets through forecasting excellence contributes to optimal inventory levels, optimized working capital, lower cost of capital, improved customer service, and reduced supply chain risk. With all these benefits to be had, why do so many business enterprises still rely on rule-of-thumb safety stock targets that manage to deliver adequate results when all the stars are lined up perfectly? One simple answer is the *historical* lack of information sharing. This cause of subpar performance can be attributed to a lack of sufficient automation. However, in recent years, the availability of automation solutions has exploded. These solutions provide the building blocks of a platform for execution that can deliver the end-to-end information transparency and velocity that is critical to the success of today's business enterprise. The challenge now is not just automation; it is process improvement, automation, integration, and standardization that are keeping today's corporations from reaping the benefits mentioned earlier.

In the context of managing enterprise risk, procurement needs to work closely with the groups directly responsible for managing different types of risks such as political and financial risk. The accounts payable (A/P) function as well as treasury should be high on this list of collaborators. These functions should align their goals and objectives and co-create reports and other information-sharing mechanisms that leverage their combined expertise to give the enterprise the means to maximize profitability. This objective can be supported directly by a well-designed and optimized platform for execution.

The greatest value added from procurement comes from the impact it can have on gross margins through direct purchasing as well as to the operating margin through indirect purchasing (to a lesser degree). Procurement's expertise in strategic sourcing, contract negotiation, and supplier relationship management is vital to the effective management of the total spend of the organization.

The specific expertise that the procurement staff needs depends greatly on the type of business and its industry. For a consumer goods manufacturing business in the beverages industry, for example, the ability to source raw materials for the production of beverages on the best possible terms would be paramount. This capability would directly impact business gross margins and give the firm either a fundamental competitive advantage or a disadvantage against its competitors. Procurement staff members who can deliver this advantage are highly prized by the businesses they work in and rightfully so.

For indirect spend, a lot of business enterprises take a less structured approach, usually not with good results. Since this category of spend is not part of COGS for a product-oriented business, there is no natural single owner of the total spend in this category. Nevertheless, it is vitally important to the overall business profitability that this spend be owned and managed under a single senior executive, preferably not the chief financial officer (CFO). The reason for having a single senior executive other than the CFO own and manage this category of spend is that it takes a lot of time and attention that the CFO does not have. The indirect spend category is filled with suppliers that are often in flux, meaning they come and go at a rate far greater than direct suppliers. The importance of managing this spend category under a single senior executive cannot be overemphasized, given that it typically represents the second largest spend area for a business. Consolidating it in this fashion can deliver these benefits:

- Smaller number of suppliers
- Greater leverage with suppliers due to spend concentration
- Greater compliance with negotiated terms
- Reduction in rogue spending
- Better visibility of the spend pipeline

These benefits accrue to the organization directly and positively impact other profitability-maximizing processes related to working capital. The overarching best practice in this regard is to consolidate and streamline the information flow throughout the end-to-end financial supply chain so that it can be available in a timely fashion to all stakeholders. The tangible benefit of implementing this best practice is maximum sustainable profitability.

Enabling Technologies

The most value that procurement can add to an enterprise, aside from its main function of purchasing of goods and services, is through the coordination of vital information related to the supply chain. The procurement function sits at the head of the pipeline of the biggest spend area in an enterprise. By establishing appropriate spend management policies and then leveraging a platform for execution that makes the supply chain information transparent and readily available to various stakeholders, both internal and external, procurement can help streamline the working capital cash flows that would result in maximizing profitability for the enterprise. In this section, we explore some of the technologies and process designs that deliver on this objective.

One of the key developments in recent years has been the enablement of efficient SCF through information technology automation, as depicted in Figure 7.1.

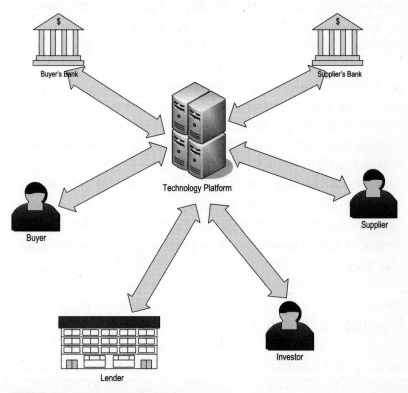

FIGURE 7.1 Supply Chain Finance

161

We now review some of the leading players in this arena. These firms provide products and services to enhance the value proposition of the procurement function by extending the scope of services that this function can provide and facilitate.

Ariba

Ariba (www.ariba.com) is a leading player in the spend management space. It provides a technology platform and services to enterprises across the globe. One of its core offerings is Ariba Buyer, which automates the full buying cycle in a secure manner. The functionality of this solution provides visibility and management of the enterprise-wide spend on products and services. The key benefits include leveraging supplier spend, managing costs, strengthened internal controls, and shorter procure-to-pay cycle times. This solution provides visibility into the entire process to all trading participants involved in the transactions. By integrating with trading partners' ERP systems, Ariba Buyer increases the velocity and value of the information throughout the financial supply chain.

One of the key benefits of this platform for procurement is its ability to encourage compliance with contracts to secure the full benefit of the negotiated terms for the buyer. It can also enable the restriction of any purchases that do not conform to the corporate policy or the terms of a specific supplier. This up-front management of procurement policies can have a significant positive influence on internal buyers while freeing the procurement staff to focus on handling any process exceptions and discovering better sourcing opportunities. From a total cost-of-ownership perspective, the solution can be delivered as installed software behind a corporate firewall, as a hosted application, or as part of an Ariba-managed service solution.

162

One of the core instruments of procurement management is a *purchase contract*. This instrument tracks the negotiated commitments and transactions between buyer and supplier. The importance of this instrument is known to almost all organizations engaged in procurement activities, but most are unable to leverage it for their benefit. Various factors combine to dilute the value that could be derived from purchase contracts, including:

- Poor contract visibility and long purchase requisition approval cycles, leading to value-destroying rogue purchasing transactions
- Inconsistent and duplicate contract creation
- Preferred supplier bypass
- Missed discounts and rebates

The most immediate impact of these deficiencies is a loss of economic value; a more troubling challenge is the risk exposure created through weakened controls and compliance.

Ariba Contract Management solves these problems. It streamlines and automates the contracting process and improves the visibility into existing agreements. It supports line-item-level price compliance with Ariba Procurement solutions to support contract compliance in the requisitioning and invoicing processes. The benefits of the Ariba platform lie in the greatly increased velocity, transparency, and integration of the various information flows that are cross-functional in nature and critical to the effective management of working capital. The procurement function can benefit greatly from using a platform such as Ariba to add real and immediate value to the enterprise by contributing to its goal of maximizing profitability.

Ariba also plays a key role in the SCF arena by partnering with the Receivables Exchange, an entity we explored in Chapter 6. Through this combination of procurement and SCF solutions, Ariba enables forward-thinking organizations to achieve their goal of increasing shareholder value by maximizing profitability.

Basware

Basware (www.basware.com) aims to improve and automate the often time-consuming and error-prone manual procurement processes that result in poor spend visibility, lack of process control, and wasted opportunities for leveraging corporate spend. Its vehicle for helping organizations achieve this goal is its e-procurement platform, Basware Purchase Management (PM). This platform automates the enterprise purchasing processes by providing a cost-efficient way to manage and control the requisitioning, approval, and ordering processes. The solution enables requisitioning and approval work flow automation and facilitates efficient ordering and receiving of goods. The purchasing can be plan based, based on product catalogs, or based on external punch-out or free-text requisitioning.

In addition, Basware's suite of products includes solutions that address the needs of various facets of the procurement process, including contract management, bidding, order matching for invoice approval, and reporting.

PrimeRevenue

PrimeRevenue (www.primerevenue.com) enables balancing of the procurement and corporate finance objectives when they are not aligned due to tactical reasons. Often procurement may be looking for discounts while finance may want to extend days payables outstanding, two goals that are orthogonal in the traditional sense. PrimeRevenue enables buyers to upload approved invoices for suppliers onto its system where suppliers can view the amounts and payment dates. Supplier can then decide to wait for payment or trade the receivables for advance payment. If a supplier wants to trade its receivables, third-party financial institutions can buy the receivables through a market-based bidding process. This process enables suppliers to get needed cash flow, investors make a profit, and buyers can extend payment terms. This is a true win-win approach to SCF.

Orbian

Financial supply chain management has taken front row on the agendas of senior corporate management across the globe in this most recent economic downturn. As credit markets have dried up and sources of funding working capital have virtually disappeared overnight, far too many businesses have been caught off guard and unprepared to deal with the crisis. The number of corporate casualties of this financial storm is high and still being counted.

Following the lead of proactive managements at leading enterprises, an increasingly greater number of companies have realized that a critical factor in the overall economic health of a business enterprise is active financial supply chain management. There is an intense and growing focus on creating an automated and more efficient payment and settlement process along with the ability to access integrated SCF programs. Orbian (www.orbian.com) enables both ends of the supply chain, buyers and suppliers, to simplify their processes, lower costs, and manage their relationships more effectively, resulting in maximum profitability.

Orbian excels at enabling high levels of cost-efficient financing for supply chain trading partners. Combining its proprietary technology platform with its network of partner banks, it can make available funding programs to grease the wheels of the corporate working capital train in a way not possible before.

Lessons for procurement to deal with tough economic times and prosper in good:

- It all begins with supplier relationships.
- Take a systems approach, not one that sacrifices long-term goals for short-term tactical gains.
- Don't focus on price alone; look at the total cost of ownership.
- Analyze the supply chain risk at all levels.
- Invest in your staff through frequent training.
- Leverage lean and six sigma methodologies for process improvement.

Procurement function has a key role to play in working capital optimization. The resulting improvement in key financial ratios can increase vendor and investor confidence. Increased vendor confidence may lead to favorable pricing positions and payment terms, resulting in lower operating costs and more available cash to invest in growth.

Case Study

A medium-size manufacturing organization was facing significant pressures from both market share and cost perspectives. The long-standing processes and systems that enabled them were fragmented with no direct visibility of the end-to-end, procure-to-pay process pipeline. A consulting firm was engaged to help analyze the situation and provide fresh insights for turning it around.

Through process mapping, analysis, and benchmarking, the team recommended that the two new initiatives be undertaken:

1. Launch a procurement card (P-card) program for high-volume, low-value purchases.

2. Utilize an e-procurement platform

The P-card program was rolled out with the help of one of the partner banks. It took 12 weeks to roll out and reduced the workload in procurement, accounts payable, treasury, and midlevel management due to the automation of approval, accruals, and reconciliation. It also provided a significant amount of cash rebate opportunity to the organization due to a consolidation of indirect spend on the P-card platform.

The e-procurement platform provided these key functions to drive efficiencies throughout the process:

- Self-service procurement
- Plan-driven procurement
- Catalog management
- Centralized contract management
- Purchasing analytics

The new platform provided built-in controls for spend management by limiting the types and amounts of the products that employees could order and approve. This freed and enabled the procurement staff to focus on value-adding tasks related to contract negotiations, strategic sourcing, and supplier relationships, all of which improved the cost side of the equation.

One of the key steps taken as part of the initiative was the rationalization of the vendor master database. The old system contained well over 75,000 supplier records with

(Continued)

167

multiple entries for several suppliers and no total supplier spend analysis. The substantially lower number of records in the new platform and the lower number of actual suppliers based on spend analysis resulted in increasing the quality of those suppliers and their relationships with the organization. A supplier on-boarding process was also put in place to ensure that the chaos of the old system would not be re-created in the new environment over time. The system automates and enforces this on-boarding process, thus providing stronger Sarbanes-Oxley compliance.

The e-procurement module was rolled out to all corporate and field purchasers with a mandate that all purchases must be made through the system. Purchases made through this new system were in excess of $65 million in the first year after implementation, generating incremental net savings of over $3 million. This initiative could not have been successful without these three factors:

1. Strong support from senior executive management
2. Well-organized and executed change management
3. Extensive user involvement and training

Conclusion

Direct and indirect procurement make up the biggest areas of cash outflows for the vast majority of organizations. Whether the organization's business is products or services, these two components of the income statement consume most of its cash outlays. Not managing these components carefully and creatively means loss of material value to the organization and its shareholders.

Leading organizations go beyond strategic sourcing and look at the end-to-end procure-to-pay process. Outwardly facing, they engage their suppliers closely in the forecasting and scheduling activities while negotiating on price and terms that best serve their own needs. In the organizations themselves, they understand the indispensable need for integrating procurement information flows and controls with finance, specifically with accounts payable and treasury processes. This holistic approach to orchestrating the entire procure-to-pay process moves organizations toward a streamlined, automated, integrated, and standardized platform for execution that delivers predictable and sustainable profitability for years to come.

Note

1 Ehap Sabri, Arun Gupta, and Michael Beitler, *Purchase Order Management Best Practices* (Fort Lauderdale, FL: J. Ross Publishing, 2007). William Copacino, *Supply Chain Management* (Boca Raton, FL: CRC Press, 1997).

CHAPTER 8

Optimizing Treasury Operations

There is nothing so useless as doing efficiently that which should not be done at all.

—Peter Drucker

Corporate finance deals with the financial decisions and the tool and analysis methods needed for making these decisions. The objective in this regard is to maximize corporate value while at the same time managing and minimizing the financial risk for the organization.

The decisions that treasury is involved in have two forms: long-term capital decisions and short-term decisions. For the long-term decisions, the analysis is about which projects receive funding and how to provide that funding, whether with debt or equity capital. It also includes decisions about dividends policy. The short-term decisions are concerned with current assets and liabilities. The focus in this regard is on working capital management in all its forms. The ultimate goal is managing cash, inventories, and short-term borrowing and lending in a manner that supports the organization's strategy for maximizing profitability while carefully balancing its liquidity needs.

This chapter focuses primarily on this latter aspect of the role of treasury function: working capital optimization.

Treasury operations comprise the nerve center of a corporation's working capital management. This area of the business not only ensures the availability of sufficient liquidity to support daily business operations; it also maximizes the use of surplus cash and plans for covering any cash shortfalls. It depends heavily on the information that originates in accounts payable (A/P), accounts receivable (A/R), and purchasing, among others.

There is a fundamental difference between accounting and finance that is often not understood by people in business. At the most basic level, accounting is about recording and reporting the historical financial activities of the business. Finance, however, is concerned with planning and projecting the future financial activities of the business. The difference is akin to looking out the front windshield (finance) and looking out the rear windshield (accounting). Understanding this difference is crucial to structuring an efficient and effective financial back office. This subtle but fundamental and very important distinction between accounting and finance has an impact on how professionals in each field approach business challenges and opportunities. In particular, at the leadership level where policies and organizational structural decisions are made, the background of the leader in one area or the other has a great deal of influence on the organization's efficiency. The acknowledgment of this fact is revealed in the relative percentage of new chief financial officer (CFO) appointments in the United States during the dot-com era, where a vast majority of these individuals had a finance background and had previously held positions in treasury. After the passage of the Sarbanes-Oxley Act of 2002 (SOX) in the aftermath of the WorldCom scandal and others, a vast majority of the CFO appointments were individuals who had CPA certifications. Their deep expertise in generally accepted accounting principles (GAAP) was deemed critical in ensuring SOX compliance at the organizational level. These CFOs primarily came from the role of controller. The tide is turning once again in the favor of treasury professionals as the world economy struggles to recover from a devastating financial crisis.

Finance at its core includes these five roles:

1. **Accounting.** Record and report on the financial activities of the business.
2. **Funding.** Raise capital to fund value creating projects.
3. **Capital budgeting.** Prioritize the funding for projects for value creation.
4. **Financial planning.** Analyze and forecast funding needs.
5. **Financial risk management.** Manage the financial risks due to currency exchange rates, interest rates, and other economic factors.

Treasury is a part of the finance function. Its responsibilities are closely linked to the business operating cycle, which has these phases:

- Acquire materials or resources.
- Convert materials into goods or resources into services.
- Sell goods or services.
- Collect payment for goods or services sold.

Given its close alignment with the entire business cycle, treasury's key objectives are to:

- **Maintain liquidity.** Ensure sufficient cash is on hand to pay short-term obligations
- **Optimize cash resources.** Balance the need to maintain liquidity and minimize idle cash by investing excess cash or paying down debt.

- **Establish and maintain access to short-term financing.** Manage banking relationships to have sufficient lines of credit available at a low cost of funds to close the working capital gap.
- **Maintain access to medium- and long-term financing.** Leverage the capital markets to secure debt and equity financing, as appropriate for the target capital structure.
- **Manage risk.** Monitor, plan for, and react to the financial risks due to current exchange rates, interest rates, and other financial factors.
- **Maintain shareholder relationships.** Sometimes treasury is responsible for maintaining effective communications with the shareholder community, but many large business enterprises have a separate group within the finance function dedicated to this role.
- **Share financial information.** Provide key financial information to management and financial institutions.

As we can see, treasury has a key role to play in any business enterprise of significant size. This entails a wide array of responsibilities and objectives. Figure 8.1 depicts treasury's central pivotal role.

For the purpose of this book, we focus only on those aspects of the treasury function that deal with cash flows and their impact on working capital. The types of cash flows treasury directly deals with include:

- **Cash inflows.** Cash received from operating, financing, and investing activities.
- **Concentration and liquidity management flows.** The activities surrounding moving cash between business units and across company bank accounts.

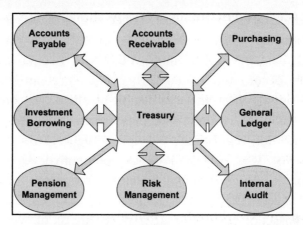

FIGURE 8.1 Central Role of Treasury

- **Cash outflows.** The cash used to pay obligations, such as employees, suppliers, and tax authorities, and for short-term investing activities.

Our focus here is on the processes and enabling technologies that engender best practices. We leave other aspects of treasury best practices, such as bank and shareholder relationship management, to other books. The reason for this segmentation of focus is that we are interested in defining a complete financial back-office platform for execution that would engender maximum profitability for a business enterprise. Softer elements, such as relationship management, are not the domain of such a platform; they require an experienced human touch.

Implications of Treasury Effectiveness

There are substantial benefits for a company in improving its treasury and working capital processes. It gains greater operational effectiveness in AP and AP from faster processing times and improves the ability of its clerical personnel to provide value-added activities. In A/R, collection rates increase and bad-debt write-offs decrease, while in A/P, data errors are reduced, data integrity is improved, fewer overpayments to suppliers occur, and overall processing costs are reduced. Process optimization and automation result in the company's greater ability to comply with increasingly stringent government reporting regulations, develop a higher level of stakeholder trust, and gain a stronger competitive edge in the marketplace. For the global business enterprise, the results include a reduction in foreign exchange risk exposure and lower transaction costs. Treasury reduces its risk of overfunding payables and maintaining excess balances, increases its access to funds to help the company sustain operations or expand the business, and enhances its control over investment risk. Treasury also sees other benefits, including lower bank charges, better access to desirable financing instruments and rates, improved information flow with banking partners, and increased leverage in bank negotiations. Overall, the company gains more opportunities to improve liquidity and return on idle working capital and lowers the costs of its financial processes. This creates more available cash for either investing in the business or returning to shareholders as dividends.

In a global economy, companies are constantly looking for a differentiator that would enable a sustainable competitive advantage. A majority of companies take the path of innovation and bring new technologies or unique product or service offerings to the market. Companies that use best practices in their financial back office gain a sustainable advantage, typically with a much lower investment and far more reliable return on investment, by creating stronger and more efficient core business processes. These companies aim to enhance the value of their treasury operation by lowering costs and freeing up resources for investment through better working capital management.

By achieving this goal of optimizing treasury operations, they realize benefits that include the ability to:

- Strengthen cash flow.
- Settle payments quickly.
- Reduce working capital liabilities.
- Negotiate favorable payment terms with suppliers.
- Establish clear accountability in A/P and A/R.
- Increase the value of collections personnel.
- Gather better information to support decision making.

When we look at the business-to-business (B2B) landscape in the United States and the rest of the globe, we see an ocean of paper. An overwhelming majority of B2B transaction entail the creation, exchange, processing, archiving, and retrieval of paper documents. Processes have been built around these paper documents with a perplexing level of complexity. One of the side effects of these paper-laden processes is the existence of various forms of float. Float is the time interval between the start and completion of a specific phase or process along the cash flow timeline. Managing these various forms of float takes time away from other value-adding activities, such as analysis and planning. Some of the key types of float are:

- Payment float
- Disbursement float
- Invoicing float
- Collection float

All this float has to be carefully planned for, monitored, managed, and reacted to. The time and resources this consumes and the fragile alignment of the functional groups involved makes this method of managing working capital far from efficient. At the core of this problem lie the various paper documents and the processes built around them. Companies have learned to shorten all types of float associated with paper-based collections and to lengthen all types of float associated with paper-based disbursements. While these float management practices give the illusion of benefit to the organization using them, in reality they are a zero-sum game with no real winners. For every action on the part of a buyer to extend float (e.g., controlled disbursement), there is an equal and opposite reaction by the seller to reduce it (e.g., lockbox). As discussed in Chapter 5, the buyer's lengthening of its payables results in the lengthening of the seller's receivables. This cost of doing business for the seller will inevitably be embedded in the price, quality, and service it delivers to its buyers. A better approach now being followed by leading organizations entails working closely with upstream and downstream partners in the end-to-end supply chain to drive down costs.

The processes that have a touch point with the value-chain partners on the operational level produce critical information that is used in treasury (A/P, procurement). Additionally, the transactional information between the organization and its customers also flows into the treasury's area of concern (A/R). This information has patterns that change greatly due to daily business operations and is used for managing working capital. The faster this information can reach treasury and the more accurate it is, the better is treasury's ability to manage working capital, liquidity, and cash. To achieve this effective management of working capital and liquidity, however, requires a carefully designed organizational structure supported and enabled by an equally well-designed platform for execution. The work, however, is not done once these elements are in place. They have to be monitored frequently and adjusted and improved as business environments, internal and external, change. The dynamic globalized competitive landscape in which today's business enterprise operates does not allow one the luxury of sitting back for long. Organizations that take their eye off of the vital task of working capital process optimization and stop investing in the processes that affect treasury do so at the cost of reduced profitability and even liquidity.

Best Practices

In the realm of treasury management, the best practices in the area of processes and enabling technologies are geared toward forging win-win strategic partnerships between trading partners. Due to the dependence of treasury on other functions for information that impacts working capital (A/R, A/P, purchasing), utilization of best practices in these other functions leads to enabling the best practices within treasury. The biggest benefit treasury gains is that it can allocate more of its time to analysis and activities that deal with the markets instead of spending too much time on cash forecasting. Although cash forecasting is very important, it can be automated to a great degree with a higher level of accuracy.

Dividing best practices across functional areas, we have these broad categories:

- Accounts receivable or payment processing
  Goal: Get the cash in as fast as possible.
- Accounts payable/disbursements
  Goal: Release the cash at the last possible moment.
- Investing
  Goal: Earn maximum return on excess cash while managing risk.

Just as in business overall, where the focus has shifted from the end of the operating cycle to the beginning, resulting in practices such as just-in-time inventory and supply chain management, treasury operations in leading companies are increasingly moving toward more efficient and secure forms of information exchange with trading partners and customers. This includes funds movement such as automated clearinghouse payments, billing information in A/R, invoice information in A/P, and purchasing commitments in purchasing functions. The earlier in the cycle this information becomes visible to treasury, the better able it is to plan, project, analyze, and react to the various financial risks that it has to manage.

Treasury functions at most top-performing companies across a diverse array of industries have a high percentage of electronic payments rather than paper ones. This is especially true of many successful multinational companies that primarily conduct business in Europe. Treasurers at the leading companies are using lockboxes and new technologies, such as check imaging, to accelerate cash collection. In cases where technology solutions prove to be too expensive, they try to ensure that payments are processed automatically using daily consolidation of funds to one or a few accounts (with minimal manual intervention). For these treasurers, a high percentage of check conversion will improve most collection and concentration processes. In addition, several top treasury services banks now offer check imaging as well as controlled disbursement accounts with full reconciliation services. Most businesses now use positive pay services and have in place platforms and processes such that checks are not manually generated. An occasional manual check is still required by these businesses.

In order for treasury to mitigate liquidity risk in terms of cash shortage, it is vital to streamline the processes and platforms around control, access, and forecasting. The goal here is to achieve visibility of cash flows across the enterprise because a firm needs to know where its cash is and how to get its hands on it when it needs it; it also must be prepared for future credit or cash flow problems. For businesses, it is

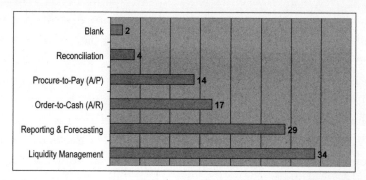

FIGURE 8.2 Highest Potential for Improvement in Cash Management

now more important than ever to secure the availability of future liquidity. A 2008 cross-industry survey found that liquidity management topped the list in terms of areas for improving cash management within an organization, according to 34% of the corporate entities surveyed (see Figure 8.2).

In a previous survey, corporate respondents indicated that the process with the highest potential for improving cash management within their organization was cash flow forecasting; by 2008, the respondents said the highest potential for improvement lies in the processes around liquidity management. This shift is due primarily to the severe impact of the credit crunch, which has brought to the forefront the importance of efficient cash management. Cash flow forecasting remains a priority as it supports the goal of liquidity management. Without accurate cash forecasts, treasury is forced to fly blind in terms of balancing the needs to minimize idle cash and maintain adequate liquidity. The main barriers to accurate cash forecasts are inaccurate sales projections and a lack of integration between internal systems. Limited availability of resources and a lack of interdepartmental communication are also leading factors in this regard.

Excel is a great tool for many purposes, and most people in the business world are familiar with it. It is also inexpensive and easy to learn. However, the manual process of creating and updating spreadsheets and then moving data around from one spreadsheet to another and eventually, perhaps, loading it into a financial system such as an enterprise resource planning (ERP) platform is fraught with errors. It is true that treasurers can achieve accurate cash forecasts with Excel, but the approach is very time consuming and requires multiple checks for accuracy due to the potential for human error. In addition, Excel has its own limitations, which at times introduce data errors that are difficult to detect and correct. Although today more and more business enterprises are moving toward using a module in the company's ERP system or a specialized stand-alone software package from a third party, many continue to use spreadsheet models. Overall, however, the trend is definitely toward a move away from Excel spreadsheets for cash forecasting.

Let's face it: We in business management love spreadsheets, and treasury is no exception. It is not that spreadsheets are inherently a bad thing. They have a place in certain situations and processes. The main problem is that companies that rely heavily on spreadsheets in core processes have a weaker process overall. It is this weakness that makes the financial back office less efficient and effective, and it results in a material impact on enterprise profitability, not to mention the issues with internal controls and their impact on SOX compliance.

The global economic crisis that began in late 2007 has made cash a scarce and expensive resource. It is no wonder then that there is currently a tremendous focus on liquidity management. Liquidity management and cash flow forecasting are closely linked; a business cannot focus on one without attending to the other. Since cash flow is vital to business profitability and survival, cash forecasting should always be a top priority, no matter what the economy and the markets do. Treasuries at leading companies that have invested in the infrastructure to enable information integration and transparency across the enterprise have been able to reduce the cost of borrowing through in-house banking activities. Not only has this allowed the companies to save significant sums in cost of debt, but it also has allowed them to help strategic suppliers that did not have access to credit while generating a return for their own organization. What they have adopted is now becoming better known as supply chain finance. Here trading partners as well as intermediary banks buy and sell the obligations created between trading partners. This trend has created opportunities for investors at large, in the form of the Receivables Exchange (www.receivablesxchange.com). As mentioned in Chapter 6, holders of accounts receivables obligations (B2B sellers) sell their receivables in an online marketplace to investors that have chosen to participate. This channel has benefited all these parties:

- **B2B buyer.** The party who will pay the invoice
- **B2B seller.** The party to whom the invoice will be paid
- **Investor.** A third party interested in a low-risk return

As opposed to the practice of factoring, which uses the credit of the A/R holder to determine the discount rate for the receivable, this channel uses the credit rating of the entity that owns the corresponding A/P obligation. In addition, this channel is market based and therefore benefits the seller of the receivable in the form of lower discount rates due to the open competitive process. In factoring, the discount rates are truly what is called "load sharking" on the consumer side.

Based on what has been presented thus far, we can see how important it is that the A/P, A/R, and procurement systems be integrated into the "treasury dashboard" to provide the extremely important information transparency that is crucial to meeting the firm's stated objectives. It is unfortunate and to the

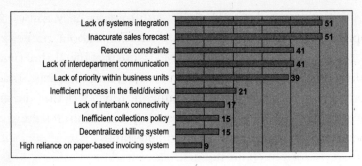

FIGURE 8.3 Barriers to Accurate Cash Flow Forecasting

detriment of a vast majority of the business enterprises of all sizes today that they do not have a sufficient level of integration between these systems at the information and transaction level. Without this integration, it is impossible to build efficient processes that enhance value creation and profitability. In terms of working capital, the majority of companies surveyed consider the quality of their core financial back-office processes (purchase to pay, order to cash, and inventory cycle) to be average or good; few describing these processes as best practice. The results of this survey are captured in Figure 8.3.

The key obstacles standing in the way of optimizing working capital were identified as:

- Cash forecasting
- Data collection, analysis, and integration
- Cash concentration
- Inventory management
- Accounts receivable
- Accounts payable
- Internal communication

When we recognize the fact that working capital is one of the most process-oriented areas within any organization, we

184

can begin to understand the need to take a step-by-step approach and ask basic yet vital questions about processes, such as the way incoming invoices are handled, the touch points involved in sending out an invoice, and the costs associated with disbursements, to name a few. Working capital improvement is all about process optimization resulting in operational excellence across the enterprise.

Create Clearly Defined Investment Policies

Treasury's goal for investing excess cash is to improve returns on the cash invested. This, however, must be balanced against the need for managing the risk inherent in investing. Companies that lose sight of their investment policies and pursue maximum return on their cash investment have sustained significant losses. This risk is greatest when a firm invests in potentially volatile investments that could quickly lose value or even become worthless. It is a best practice to do the work of clearly defining goals and guidelines before investing funds to maximize investment returns. Having established these guidelines and objectives, companies can better balance risk thresholds and liquidity needs against optimal costs of investing to achieve the best possible results. In order to manage risk and minimize idle cash resources, companies should move idle funds daily to income-generating accounts. In cases where banks do not pay interest on demand deposit accounts, companies should use sweep accounts and zero-balance accounts to avoid penalties and maximize interest earnings. Doing this also helps a company avoid or minimize overdrafts in cases where banks impose major fees for this service. Most companies can and should leverage web-based treasury management technology to monitor investments and assess the credit risk associated with investment issuers. Companies that do not have the resources or the expertise to actively manage their portfolio should outsource the investment task. Many companies do so simply to avoid missing investment opportunities.

Consolidate Banking Partners

As a best practice, companies consolidate their financial accounts using a few carefully chosen banks. This engenders a close relationship between the company and the banking partners on which the company can rely without creating a dependence on a single bank. If one of the banks has difficulties, the company can continue with uninterrupted service using another banking partner. This best practice has shown its value in the most recent credit crunch, which ensued after the collapse of some of the biggest and best-known banks in the United States. Having a smaller number of banking partners also gives the company considerable advantage in negotiating with the banks as it can use the leverage created by the concentration of its business with a small number of banks. The treasury in the company can use scorecards to better assess bank services, line by line, to compare pricing. Sharing the scorecard with the banking partners lets them know how they compare to their competitors, and companies gain leverage to negotiate more favorable bank fees and preferential services. This is an important consideration since, increasingly, price surpasses service as the criterion by which companies shop for cash management banks.

Another benefit of bank accounts consolidation is lower transaction costs and improved process efficiency. A treasurer managing just a few banking relationships can consolidate cash management services to obtain lower fees and improve the timeliness and quality of data concerning the company's global cash position. When shopping for a banking partner, companies should thoroughly review cash management needs by gathering input from all departments the bank may have an

186

impact on. An evaluation of how well current banking needs are met and the expectations for future needs is also crucial in this regard. A team should be created that includes financial experts led by a banking relationship manager to analyze how well potential banks will meet the specific needs of the company and create detailed service-level agreements with chosen banks.

Strive to Reduce the Cost of Capital on an Ongoing Basis

Capital structure theory strives to minimize the cost of capital for a business enterprise. It achieves this by balancing the level of debt and equity on the company's balance sheet. Other, less obvious factors exist that indirectly influence a company's weighted average cost of capital (WACC). It is prudent to keep these factors at the forefront of thought. Their effect, while not factored into capital structure decisions, is nevertheless real on the actual realized WACC for the business enterprise. Some of these factors include:

- Financial transparency
- Corporate governance
- Treasury efficiency

Keeping the financial stakeholders apprised of the company's goals, strategy, plans, performance, and any relevant nonfinancial information on an ongoing basis should be a high-priority task for the financial managers. This information provides the necessary context for the company's external financial reports and results in the company's ability to consistently attract capital because investors naturally gravitate toward companies they understand.

A company with a robust and effective investor relations program can reduce investor uncertainty, attract additional investors, and reduce the cost of capital by explaining and putting into context the company's value drivers and goals.

Explore Alternative Financing Sources

Most companies are familiar with and rely on traditional sources of capital, such as commercial banks, debt and equity markets, institutional investors, and private equity firms. In some circumstances, these sources of capital may view the company as less attractive for investment. The consolidation in banking industry, for example, has enabled the banks to be selective, depriving many businesses of sources of funding that were once reliable. Furthermore, the imposition of certain regulations prevents banks from lending to companies whose debt-to-equity ratios do not meet the rather conservative limits used by the banks. The bank lending business also is cyclical, which means that many credit-seeking companies may be left without liquidity during hard cycles due to the differences in their business cycle and that of the banks.

In order to overcome these hurdles, leading business enterprises engage in a practice of regularly looking for and analyzing alternative funding sources. They look ahead to their future funding needs and keep an eye on emerging funding sources so that they will be better able to identify available sources when they are needed. On their funding sources radar, they keep a close eye on sources of nontraditional capital so that they can obtain funding readily during times of tight credit, stock market slumps, or industry downturns. It is also a common practice of these leading companies to partner with other companies, place assets as collateral, and squeeze credit from suppliers and vendors. Doing this enables the companies to retain the liquidity required to remain competitive during difficult periods. Among the best practices used by these leading business enterprises is the formation of a joint venture or strategic partnership to pool the financial resources and spread risk for mutual benefit. These relationships typically involve a significant investment by a larger company in a smaller one. The arrangement may be between a customer and a supplier or between two companies with complementary strengths in the same business.

The advantages of joint ventures and strategic partnerships include:

- Access to financing that might not be available normally.
- Partnering with an entity that understands the true market value of the company.
- Securing an equity price better than what the open market would bear.
- Protection from takeovers.

Automate Financial Reporting

The financial reporting process is another area where leading companies have realized the benefits of automating. By reengineering the process to eliminate the use of spreadsheets, they have gained efficiencies in the treasury system and eliminated the risk involved in spreadsheet accounting. Incompatible and inefficient financial reporting systems can cause budget shortfalls, audit exposure, loss of stakeholder trust, and even government intervention. Web-enabled technological alternatives, such as eXtensible Business Reporting Language (XBRL), allow users to compile and exchange financial information regardless of their technology platform. This standards-based method for generating accurate, complex financial deliverables is technology platform neutral. These automation solutions can facilitate collaboration and data sharing, resulting in faster and more accurate financial reporting, more effective reporting controls, and cost savings in every area of cash management. Treasury professionals can focus on relationships with banks, trading partners, and customers. Users across the enterprise gain real-time access to accurate business transaction activity. Together, these benefits promote better overall financial decision making and help a company gain or maintain a competitive edge.

Monitor Financial Exposure

When high-risk investment strategies, such as hedging, are utilized, treasury should monitor financial exposure for each transaction on a daily basis. Frequent marking of the value of each hedging transaction at specific times during the day enables treasury to stay on top of market risk exposures. Doing this is achievable with today's state-of-the-art and affordable information systems, which provide, at a minimum, free and unrestricted access to accurate, real-time data. For custom-ized trading simulations and accounting requirements, special-ized systems are available as well. To be effective, a monthly reporting package should include exposure details for cur-rency, interest rate, and commodities trading. The package should also contain actual hedge coverage levels compared to targets, levels of policy compliance, and risk analysis results for each area. The quarterly report that treasury creates consolidates these monthly reports to provide a risk report for distribution to senior financial management, corporate planning personnel, operating unit managers, and the company's risk committee.

Technology-enabled trading simulations and audit tools are invaluable for monitoring the investment portfolio. With simula-tions, treasury staff can see how hedging positions would perform under all market conditions and forecast funding requirements by currency. The staff can be alerted by audits to potential for losses or failures so they can make prompt process evaluations to prevent future problems. Treasury best practices include internal and external audits to focus attention on risk management activities and the level of compliance with company risk policies and external financial regulations. Data integrity and internal controls can be improved, and compliance with government mandates can be ensured through regular internal auditing. Equally important is the use of periodic and spot audits by personnel outside the financial risk management function. This provides an independent and unbiased appraisal of risk management practices on a continuing basis.

Leverage a Centralized Cash Management Structure

For large multinational enterprises, the structure of global cash management operation has two levels. The first level deals with the needs of the local country of operation of the business unit or division. With a few differences, this scenario also applies to firms that do not have multinational operations. For these firms, the cash management system is focused on addressing standard treasury functions, such as collections within the home country. This level has a cash management function in each country. On the second level, a network connects local systems and manages various currencies while integrating cash management with functions such as purchasing, sales, and accounting. Due to the fact that the complexity of conditions that require a centralized cash management function varies across countries, the degree of centralization is matched to the company's specific needs. These tools are available to facilitate this matching of the company's needs for centralization:

- Multicurrency accounts
- Netting
- Currency pooling
- Cross-border pooling
- Centralized funding
- Global treasury centers

The best approach to centralizing cross-border treasury operations or cash management activities is to do it in phases. Many companies that have implemented this best practice successfully show that it is best either to centralize within each country before centralizing cross-border activities or to centralize cross-border activities before centralizing operations within each country. What is done first depends on the specific needs of each company. To reduce funds movement, it is best to keep physical cross-border transfers of funds to a minimum, using multicurrency accounts, netting, and pooling instead. The approach most often taken is to purchase international cash netting services from banks to lower transaction fees and reduce foreign exchange expenses. This approach reduces the transfer of funds between subsidiaries to a net amount. In addition, companies should also establish payment factories (centralized disbursement function) within the company to manage accounts payable for their subsidiaries. The use of payment factories enables the company to net and bundle payments, lowering the number and cost of transactions. (See Figure 8.4.)

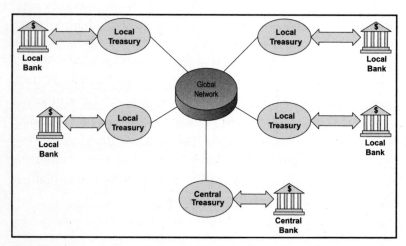

FIGURE 8.4 Centralized Treasury Configuration

Enabling Technologies

Most of the best practices mentioned earlier that are process-oriented can be enabled through the implementation of a carefully chosen platform for execution. This platform can be a single system or a collection of integrated components that work together to provide transaction automation and velocity, information availability and transparency, and rules-based process execution and alerts.

While managing the daily cash position has long been the primary focus of the typical treasury function, when treasury goes beyond this narrow focus, it adds real value to the enterprise. With the new enabling technologies and especially those that leverage the Internet to provide low-cost ubiquitous access to information, treasury can expand its focus by utilizing expedited data gathering, compilation, and analysis. The higher velocity of this critical internal and market information results in increased accuracy in forecasting, reduced borrowing expenses, improved short-term investment returns, and improved management reporting.

One thing that can be guaranteed about treasury management solutions: Like Chicago commuter trains, there will most likely be another one coming along in a few minutes. Making a choice between an ERP treasury module and a treasury management system (TMS) from a particular vendor can easily consume weeks and even months in evaluating and comparing options. Many companies, after making a selection by investing significant time and effort, have found that even before the system is implemented, there are new products and features on the market that beg consideration.

ERP Platform Treasury Modules

Almost all of the leading ERP systems today offer a treasury management module with varying levels of functionality and integration capabilities. We will not go into the details of any specific treasury module here; rather, we will discuss the pros and cons of this category of solution.

A vast majority of medium to large business enterprises utilize an ERP system. At the lower end of the cost and functionality spectrum are platforms such as Microsoft Dynamics (www.microsoft.com) and Epicor (www.epicor.com); at the upper end are systems from Oracle (www.oracle.com) and SAP (www.sap.com). By no means is this a complete listing; there are many other providers at each end of the spectrum and in between. For an organization that has already invested in an ERP platform, it makes sense in most cases to use the treasury module that is part of the platform. The only case where this may not apply is when the ERP platform does not have a treasury module or the functionality of the module is insufficient for the needs of the organization. Seldom is an ERP system chosen for its treasury module's capabilities. In their order of importance, the selection criteria in general would be:

- General ledger functionality
- Cost
- Financial reporting
- Performance
- Ease of use
- Interoperability (interfacing with other systems for data exchange)

These systems are most suitable from a cost-benefit viewpoint when implemented with their so-called out-of-the-box functionality with a minimum configuration to accommodate the organization's business structure. Most ERP implementations have failed disastrously in the past and continue to fail when attempts are made to "customize" the ERP platform to conform to the organization's way of doing business. It is best to remember that unless an organization has created a truly best practice process, it is in its own best interest to utilize the ERP's standard implementation of the same process. The ERP platform vendors usually make a good effort at harvesting cross-industry best practices and incorporating these into their standard processes. Not following this rule results in a tremendous increase in the total cost of ownership for the ERP platform.

One of key benefits of these platforms is that they do a lot of things. The downside is that they do not do everything equally well. Some ERP platforms have a great A/P module but a lackluster fixed assets module. For an organization that is fixed asset intensive, such as a hotel chain, this can be an issue. The same applies to the capabilities of the treasury module. Not all ERPs have the same level of sophistication and flexibility in each module. In particular, the ERP platform vendor's product road map may not be in alignment with the changing needs of the organization in terms of timing, or features and capabilities. While some very large organizations have been able to influence their ERP platform vendors' product road map to suit their own requirements, this is not the case for the vast majority of the business enterprises.

As an example, most treasury functions use some form of cash pooling method. There are pros and cons with all pooling methods. Zero balancing, for instance, has become the most commonly used in part because it is supported better by most of the leading ERP platforms than other pooling methods. This limits the organization from being creative and taking advantage of other pooling methods that may be more suitable for its specific needs. In addition, as legal and tax rules become more uniform between countries, the availability of new pooling methods and their support will be dependent on the product road map and timing of the ERP platform vendor. Therefore, the existing functionality as well as the flexibility of the ERP platform should be a key selection criteria for treasury.

The treasury's primary time-critical responsibilities are to reconcile the prior-day cash balance and to prepare a daily cash position worksheet. In order to accomplish these tasks, timely access is needed to data from:

- Ledger
- Bank balances
- Cash inflows
- Cash outflows
- Maturity status of investments
- Foreign exchange rates

One of the key benefits for treasury in organizations where multiple ERP systems are in use is the ability to integrate the treasury modules across all ERP platforms. Increasingly more treasurers are looking at ERP treasury management modules that are easy to interface with other ERP modules, in order to gain a more holistic view of cash and liquidity management within their company. Although many treasurers still believe that ERP treasury modules cannot compete with the depth and breadth of functionality of a TMS specialized for this purpose, the gains in visibility can be worth the sacrifice. But even this gap in functionality appears to be narrowing. As an example, SAP and Oracle in particular have improved their ERP products to include more treasury functionality, and their products are likely to appeal to a lot more treasurers now. It is very unlikely, however, that a company would embark on a major project to switch from a TMS to an ERP treasury module unless it is running old TMS technology or a supplier has failed to meet expectations.

When looking at moving to an ERP treasury management module, treasurers need to balance their need for standardization and visibility against functionality. This is the most common point of difference between an ERP treasury management module and a TMS, aside from cost considerations and the issues surrounding system maintenance and upgrades. ERP platforms provide a compelling benefit to treasury by enabling global cash management, planning, and forecasting across the enterprise. To realize this benefit, however, all units of the enterprise must be running on the same version of the ERP platform.

Stand-alone Specialized Applications

Historically, stand-alone specialized treasury applications have been the best choice when it comes to a complete and robust set of functionality. One such technology provider is Chesapeake Systems (www.chessys.com), which provides end-to-end treasury solutions that seamlessly integrate cash management with reconciliation, account analysis, and regulatory compliance functions. With information shared across all applications, treasury staff can optimize funds management, speed up account reconciliation, and simplify compliance with audit rules and financial regulations. The resulting actionable information and productivity improvements can benefit a wide range of organizations by minimizing risk, reducing costs, and maximizing profitability. Chesapeake's SmartTreasury is a complete end-to-end treasury workstation that helps a company centralize and monitor business activity, manage cash, and forecast accurately. By seamlessly integrating cash management, reconciliation, account analysis, and compliance, it provides complete control over all treasury operations. The key benefits of this TMS include:

- Bank updating and automatic delivery of real-time information
- Reduction of manual data entry
- Automated analysis
- Accurate, real-time information
- Automation of data transfer for preparing payments and transfers

A complementary tool from Chesapeake is the Chesapeake SmartAnalysis, a sophisticated tool for analyzing commercial bank fee data across all of a company's banking relationships. Using a common format regardless of the source of data, SmartAnalysis automates the comparison of actual with expected charges, highlights discrepancies, and helps ensure that treasury can get the volume discounts it is entitled to.

Another provider of stand-alone TMS is Kyriba, which offers a full TMS with an emphasis on cash and liquidity management. Its platform utilizes the latest technologies available for infrastructure, security, and Internet deployment. This architecture provides a highly scalable service offering to the domestic and international marketplace delivered to the end users through the "Software as a Service" model (SaaS). Its solution provides transparency of daily cash and treasury management processes across the operation while enabling visibility, retention, and distribution of relevant and valuable information across the enterprise. It helps automate several of the routine daily tasks within treasury and enables straight-through processing (STP), full data integration, and several others.

Kyriba's key benefits include:

- Consolidation of enterprise-wide financial information
- Management of work flow locally, regionally, and globally
- Standardization of processes across treasury operations

- Enablement of Sarbanes-Oxley compliance
- Real-time data for investment positions, forecasts, and budgets
- Multicurrency
- Monitoring of risk exposures
- Automated bank connectivity for report capture and electronic funds transfer
- Multibank communications
- Cash flow forecasting
- Bank fee analysis
- Payments: wire, automated clearinghouse, direct debit, drafts
- Multilateral netting: intracompany and third party
- Debt/Investment
- General ledger reconciliation
- Cash positioning
- Cash pooling
- General ledger posting
- In-house banking/intercompany loans
- Bank account administration
- Foreign exchange
- User-defined reporting (e-mail and published)
- Trade execution STP

Case Study

Most large corporations still have some legacy systems around which key processes are built. One such major global enterprise decided to launch an enterprise-wide infrastructure project to standardize end-to-end business processes on a single instance of an ERP platform. It also decided to implement a network of regional shared service

(Continued)

centers that gave its treasury function a unique opportunity to work with the local subsidiaries to define and implement a new global vision for treasury. Treasury created a road map for leveraging the best banking and technology structure to support the company in its strategic goals. One of the first decisions that treasury made was that all transactions and communication should rely on global industry standards such as SWIFTNet, SCORE, ISO 20022, Digital Identity Management, and XML. In this streamlined financial infrastructure, the global ERP system would communicate with a single instance of the treasury management system, which would communicate with the company's two primary global banks using the latest message formats. This would result in the use of a single delivery channel, a single file format, and one payment process supported by a handful of global banks. Treasury would have real-time access to bank account data in global affiliates, resulting in reduced treasury activity at subsidiaries around the world. The initial savings delivered by this strategy were in excess of $2 million in the first year and were just the beginning of much greater savings to come. These savings resulted from reduced bank fees, increased visibility of cash, and more productive deployment of available cash.

Conclusion

The transactional information that originates in multiple key financial processes converges to feed the working capital management engine of an enterprise. When designed and executed optimally in the form of a financial back-office platform for execution, this combined information is available to treasury in a timely fashion at a level of detail that enables it to make accurate cash forecasts. The accuracy of these cash forecasts not only feeds sound short-term borrowing and investing decisions to optimize working capital and liquidity but has an impact on the longer-term profitability of the enterprise.

Recognizing the importance of this ability to make information transparent at a high-velocity for the treasury, leading enterprises are steadily investing time and resources to optimize their financial back-office processes and systems. The resulting financial agility is well worth the investment with a handsome return on investment and a payback period that is shorter than most other investments these organizations can make within their own four walls.

Epilogue

Today's business environment is vastly different from what it was a few decades ago, both internally as well as externally. Internally, people's attitudes, expectations, and aspirations have evolved in a way that requires a new way of finding, hiring, training, motivating, retaining, and rewarding the indispensable human resources of an organization. Externally, the regulatory environment, information technology, speed of capital movement, makeup of shareholders and other stakeholders, and globalization together exert pressures that an organization operating under a mind-set and using processes from even a decade ago would be ill prepared to withstand without adverse consequences.

The key concepts in this book have revolved around profitability, cost, and capability. Over and over, these three things emerge as the corners of the triangle that is the ultimate battlefield for any business organization. This can be the golden triangle of long-term prosperity for those organizations that are profitability focused and not merely profits focused and the death triangle for those that have a short-term profits focus. What fate awaits an organization depends on whether and how well it balances its costs and capabilities. Focusing on this balance objectively with a touch of vision is the key to success.

It is my aim to start a dialogue that reminds leaders of corporations of all sizes to maintain a long-term profitability focus. This mind-set will naturally lead to investments in the foundational components of the business enterprise that make up its platform for execution. The resulting stable and agile internal structure will make the organization well positioned to respond to the ever-changing external environment. This gives the organization the ultimate edge with regard to its back office in a fiercely competitive marketplace where revenue growth is constantly under threat. With the back office securely operating at optimal levels, the leadership can focus on revenue-maximizing opportunities, knowing that each dollar of incremental revenue would add to the bottom line at a maximum level of profitability. The minimization of value and morale-destroying cycles of headcount expansion and reduction would make true on the passionate words of management that people are the most precious resource. In return, the organization will earn the dedication and loyalty of the staff that is critical to innovation, productivity, and profitability.

Let's begin by having a zero tolerance for inefficiency and lack of information transparency in the financial back-office processes. These processes are the arteries through which the blood of the business enterprise flows—its cash flow. Keeping them as healthy as possible is the most critical step toward sustainable maximum profitability. The only thing that stands in the way to reaping this crucial advantage is a lack of will and fear of the unknown. The lack of will most commonly is the result of either a short-term profit focus or a lack of understanding of the value in this space. The concepts of cost versus capability and platform for execution are not yet part of the day-to-day vocabulary in most organizations. This has to change if long-term sustained profitability is the goal. The other common factor plaguing organizations that have taken the bold step in this direction but then became disillusioned due to a lack of progress is a lack of experience. The myopic focus on cost alone keeps these organizations from engaging outside experts to help create the agile platform for execution mentioned throughout this book. It is not a lack of will in this case nor a lack of understanding of the value to be gained—it is simply a matter of looking at cost alone and not fully valuing the capability that would be gained as a result of the effort. In the end, it all comes down to "flawless execution" that has as its hallmark the right people with the right skills, the right processes, the right technologies, and speed.

Index

A

Accounting, 173
  purpose of, 59–60
Accounting Best Practices, 99
Accounts payable (A/P), 18, 28, 31, 51, 58,
  60, 88, xiii
  automation of invoice and remittance
    processing, 100–103
  best practices, 99–115
  case study on, 121–22
  enabling technologies, 115–21
  financial performance metrics, 23
  implications of effectiveness, 97–99
  manual invoice processing, 112
  metrics for manual, 110
  optimizing, 95–123
  semiautomated invoice processing, 113
  timing and terms to maximize cash flow,
    99–100
Accounts Payable Best Practices, 99
Accounts receivable (A/R), 18, 28, 51, 58,
  59–60, 88, xiii
  best practices, 130–36
  case study on, 143–44
  distressed and delinquent accounts,
    132–34
  enabling technologies, 137–43
  high-value transactions, 134–35
  implications of effectiveness, 126–30
  management, 18
  monetizing, 135–36
  optimizing, 125–45, 131–32
Accrued expenses (AE), 51, 56
Acid test, 53

Acquisition cost, 35
Advanced shipping notice (ASN), 104
Agency problem, 21
Agility, 4
  external factors of, 4
Alighieri, Dante, 93
Ariba, 140–41, 162–64
Assembly line, 70
Assets turnover, 16
Asset turnover ratio (A/S), 56
Automated clearinghouse (ACH), 102
Automobile industry, 69–70

B

Banking partners, consolidating, 186–87
Banking system, origins of, 46
Bank of America, 102
Bankruptcy, 8, 148
Basware, 142–43, 164
B2B buyer, 183
B2B seller, 183
Berkshire Hathaway, 22
Billing, 59
Blackstone Group, 17
Blockbuster, 44
Bossidy, Larry, 5
Bottom line, 54
Brand image deterioration, 35
Buffett, Warren, 1, 22, 35
Business competitive strategy, 32
Business enterprise
  competitive advantage of, 13
  costs incurred by, 35
  financial supply chain and, 48

internal factors of, 5–6
liquidity level of, 20
Business model, 31–32
   competitive strategy, 32
   core competencies, 32
Business non-value added, 79
Business paradigms, 58

C
Cadbury-Schweppes, 11
Capability, 27–44
   case study on, 33
   for generating profits, 27
   level of, 30
   measuring, 41–42
   strategic capabilities matrix, 29
Capacity, 31, 41
Capital
   budgeting, 173
   equity, 171
   requirements for, 13
   structure, 6
   working, 28, 50–58
Cash conversion cycle (CCC), 11, 16, 19, 57,
   58, 59, 136, 148
   components of, 12
Cash flow, 50, 51
   barriers to forecasting, 184
   timing and terms to maximize, 99–100
Cash inflows, 174
Cash management, improvement in, 181
Cash outflows, 95, 175
Cash-to-cash conversion, 19
Centralized cash management structure,
   191–92
Change, as constant, 75
Channel partners, 46
Chesapeake Systems, 197, 198
Chief financial officer (CFO), 21, 160, 172
Collection float, 177
Combined Code, 23
Competitive advantage, 6, 13
   value, 81
Competitive landscape, 4
Completion rate, 80
Complexity, 85–86
Conde Nast Portfolio, 3
Continuous process optimization, 78
Contract management, 32
Corporate governance, 24
Cost-capability optimization, xiii
Cost-cutting efforts, 96
Cost of goods sold (COGS), 9, 10, 96, 153,
   159
Cost of sales/inventory ratio, 53
Cost of sales/payables ratio, 53

Cost optimization, 83
Cost reduction, 7, 8
Costs, 27–44, 31
   acquisition, 35
   brand image deterioration, 35
   case study on, 33, 42–43
   cutting, 18
   dollar, 35
   opportunity, 35
Cost shifting, 48
Countrywide, 8
Credit cards, 60
Critical-to-return on investment (CTR), 128,
   129
Crown Zellerbach, 3
Current ratio, 52, 53
Cycle times, 84
   reduction in, 103–5

D
Days inventory outstanding (DIO), 57, 109,
   153, 155
Day's inventory ratio, 53
Days payables outstanding (DPO), 57, 96,
   97, 105, 108, 110
Day's payables ratio, 53
Day's receivable ratio, 53
Days sales outstanding (DSO), 57, 109,
   141, 144
Days working capital (DWC), 109
Debt
   requirements for, 13
   short-term, 51
Debt-to-equity ratio (D/E), 20, 56
Delinquent accounts, 132–34
Dell Computer Corporation, 29–30, 35, 56,
   58
Digital imaging, 101
Direct costs, minimization of, 8
Disbursement float, 177
Discount rate, 42
Dividend payout ratio, 55, 56
Dollar cost, 35
Dr. Pepper Snapple Group, 9, 10, 11
Drucker, Peter F., 45, 171
Dunlap, Albert John, 3, 4, 13
DuPont Chemical Company, 16, 17

E
Economic conditions, 4
Economic order quantity (EOQ), 156, 157
Economic profit (EP), 15
   negative, 36
Economic value added (EVA), 15
E-invoicing (electronic invoicing), 64, 101
   network, 121

Electronic data interchange (EDI), 116, 120, 140
Electronic invoice presentment and payment (EIPP), 101, 103, 117
Emerson, Ralph Waldo, 95
Enabling technologies, 115–21
  accounts receivable, 137–43
  Ariba, 140–41, 162–64
  Basware, 142–43, 164
  ERP modules and add-ons, 119–20
  ERP platform treasury modules, 194–97
  network approach, 120–21
  OB10, 141–42
  Orbian, 165–66
  PrimeRevenue, 164–65
  for purchasing, 160–66
  stand-alone applications, 119
  stand-alone specialized applications, 197–99
  for treasury operations, 193–99
End-to-end execution time, 84
Enron, 14, 15, 22
Enterprise resource planning (ERP), 32, 47, 87, 89, 116, 156, 182
  modules and add-ons, 119–20
  platform treasury modules, 194–97
Enterprise value creation, 8
ePayables (electronic payables), 64
Equity capital, 171
Error rates, 85
  reduction in, 103–5
Evaluated receipts settlement (ERS), 102, 103–5
  process flow, 106
  for purchase order invoices, 107
Execution: The Discipline of Getting Things Done (Bossidy), 5
Expenses, accrued, 51, 56
Extensible Business Reporting Language (XBRL), 189

F
FedEx, 42–43
Finance, roles of, 173
Financial back-office functions, 28
Financial back-office platform for execution, 73
Financial electronic data interchange (FEDI), 103
Financial exposure, monitoring, 190–91
Financial flexibility, 19–24
Financial leverage, 16
Financial planning, 173
Financial reporting, automation, 189–90
Financial risk management, 173
Financial supply chain (FSC), 45–68, xi

case study on, 64
defined, 45–50
generic, 49
optimization, 66–67, xiii
parts of, xiii
receivables exchange in, 137
working capital, 50–58
working capital processes, 59–63
Five Force Model, 5
Float, types of, 177
Ford, Henry, 69, 70
Free capital, 58
Full-time equivalent (FTE), 76
Funding, 173

G
Gates, Bill, 69
Generally accepted accounting principles (GAAP), 172–73
General Motors, 103, 116
Global Crossing, 22
Goods
  acquisition of, 47
  movement of, 45–46
  possession of, 62
  receipt, 116
Graham, Benjamin, 1
Gross margin, 9, 10
Gross profit, 81
Growth, 19–24

H
Hardstone Group, 101
Headcount reduction, 8, xii
High-value transactions, refocus resources on, 134–35
Human labor, 70
Human resources, 18

I
Industry fundamentals, 4
Information, bidirectional flow of, 48
Information technology (IT), 18, 38, 40, 43, 72, 76, 87
Intelligent Character Recognition (ICR), 101
Interest coverage ratio, 13
Inventory, 4, 51
  just-in-time, 157
  management, 19
  turns, 153
  vendor-managed, 157
  work-in-process, 47
Investment policies, 185–86
Investors, 183
Invoices, 116
  automation of, 100–103

manual processing, 112
   semiautomated, 113
Invoicing float, 177

J
Japanese companies, 22–23, 70
Joint ventures, advantages of, 189
JP Morgan Chase, 102
Just-in-time inventory (JIT), 157

K
Key performance indicator (KPI), 17
Killen Associates, xi
Knights Templar, 46, 47

L
Lead time, 79, 83
Lean approach, principles of, 83–84
Lengthening days payables, 58
Leverage technology, 105–15
Liabilities, short-term, 13, 52
Liquidity, 19–24
   crisis, 29
   maintaining, 53–54, 173
   management, 182
   management flows, 174
   ratios, 52, 53
   working capital and, 50, 52
Little's Law, 79
Long-term financing, 174
Long-term profitability, 65
Long-term sustainable profitability, 2
Low-cost support function, 35
Lynch, Peter, 1

M
Management
   capabilities, 6
   supply chain, 47
Measurement period, 80
Microsoft Corporation, 6, 39, 52, 55

N
Negotiations, 32
Netflix, 44
Net income (NI), 54
Net present value (NPV), 33, 57
Net profit, 54
Net profit margin (NPM), 16, 54, 55, 56, 77
Net profit value (NPV), 36, 42
Network approach, 120–21
Non-value added, 79, 83, 85

O
OB10, 141–42
Offshoring, 39

Old Economy, 63
Operating model, 34, 70
   generic, 71
Operating structure, 6
Opportunity cost, 15, 35
Optical character recognition (OCR), 101
Optimization, xii
   of accounts payable, 95–123
   of accounts receivable, 125–45, 131–32
   of cash resources, 173
   continuous process, 78
   cost, 83
   cost-capability, xiii
   financial supply chain, 66–67, xiii
   pre- and post-process, 114
   process, 82, 86
   of purchasing, 147–69
   of treasury operations, 171–201
   working capital, 51
Oracle, 39, 194, 196
Orbian, 165–66
Organizational capabilities, xii
Organizational culture, 5, 6
Organizational structure, 5

P
Payment float, 177
P-card (purchasing card), 64, 102, 167
Pepsi Co., 9, 11
Perlman, Itzhak, 27
Physical supply chain, 10, 11, 47, 48, 49, xi
Plan of action, 74
Platform for execution, 8, 69–93
   case study on, 91–92
   complexity and, 85–86
   error rates and, 85
   financial back-office, 73, 91
   generic, 72
   process automation, 86–88
   process benchmarking, 74–84
   process integration, 88–89
   process optimization, 86
   process standardization, 89–90
   velocity and cycle times, 84
Polaroid, 8
Porter, Michael, 5, 6, 7
PrimeRevenue, 164–65
Prioritization, for pull system, 81
Process automation, 86–88
   approach to, 87–88
   benefits of, 86
Process benchmarking, 74–84, 166
Process efficiency, 79, 83
Process engineering, 78
Process integration, 88–89
Process optimization, 82, 86

Process standardization, 89–90
Procurement, 18, 28, 61–62. *See also*
  Purchasing
  defined, 47
Procure-to-pay (P2P), 103
Production process, 80
Profitability
  assets turnover, 16
  defined, 2–9
  economic downturn and, 7
  equation logic tree, 18
  equations, 9–19
  financial leverage, 16
  long-term, 65
  maximization, 19, 82
  net profit margin, 16
  profits *versus*, 3
  related metrics and, 9–19
  sustainable, 2, xiii
Profits, 1–26
  capabilities for generating, 27
  case study on, 24–25
  economic, 15, 36
  financial flexibility and, 19–24
  formula for, 8
  growth and, 19–24
  liquidity and, 19–24
  maximization of, 2, 69–93
  net, 54
  profitability *versus*, 3
  return on assets and, 14–15
  return on equity and, 13–14
  return on invested capital and, 15–19
  return on sales and, 11–13
  short-term, 37
Property, plant, and equipment (PP&E), 14
Prospectors, 7
Pull system, 80
  order prioritization for, 81
Purchase contract, 163
*Purchase Order Management Best
  Practices*, 152
Purchase order (PO), 60, 102, 116
  automated, 134
  evaluated receipts settlement for, 107
Purchasing, 28, 58, 88, xiii
  best practices, 152–60
  business performance and, 148
  case study on, 167–68
  enabling technologies, 160–66
  implications of effectiveness, 149–52
  optimization of, 147–69
  platform, 90
Purchasing card (P-card). *See* P-card
  (purchasing card)
Push system, 80

Q
Quality, 30–31, 41
Quick ratio, 53

R
Receivables Exchange, 136, 183
Reducing days inventory, 58
Reducing days receivables, 58
Regulatory landscape, 4
Remittance, automation of, 100–103
Research and development (R&D), 28
Return on assets (ROA), 9, 14–15, 154
  defined, 14
  ratio, 17
Return on equity (ROE), 9, 13–14, 21, 135,
  154
  defined, 13
  ratio, 55
Return on invested capital (ROIC), 9,
  15–19, 83
  defined, 15
Return on investment (ROI), 32, 33, 44,
  111
Return on sales (ROS), 9, 11–13
  definition of, 11
Revenue (R), 54
Risk management, 174
ROS. *See* Return on sales (ROS)

S
Sales, general, and administrative (SG&A),
  18
Sales/receivable ratio, 53
Sales/working capital ratio, 53
Sarbanes-Oxley Act (SOX), 23, 98, 168,
  172, 173, 199
Scandals, 23
Scott Paper, 3
Segment focus, 6
Senior management, 149
  responsibility of, 7
Shared services organization (SSO), 31
Shareholders, 21–22
  relationships, 174
Shareholder value, 1
Short-term debt, 51
Short-term financing, 174
Short-term liabilities, 13, 52
Short-term profits, 37
Six sigma techniques, 82, 111
Small and medium business (SMB), 126
Small Town USA, 37
Software as a Service model (SaaS),
  198
Soros, George, 1
Southwest Airlines, 34

Stand-alone specialized applications,
    197–99
Stock price, 7
Straight-through processing (STP), 85,
    101–2, 115, 198
Strategic capabilities matrix, 29
Strategic partnerships, advantages of, 189
Sunbeam Corporation, 3, 4, 8
Sunbeam-Oster Corporation, 3
Supply chain
    defined, 46
    financial, 45–68, xi
    management, 8, 17, 47
    physical, 10, 11, 47, 48, 49
Supply chain finance (SCF), 150, 161
Supply Chain Management, 152
Sustainable growth rate (SGR), 20, 55
    formula for, 55
Sustainable profitability, xiii
    long-term, 2

T
Tax, 18
Throughput, 30
Time value map (TVM), 78, 84
    purchase order process, 79
Timing, 99–100
Total cost of ownership (TCO), 131
Toyota Motor Company, 22, 70
Tracy, Brian, 1
Treasury, 18, 28, 88, xiii
    bill, 15
    central role of, 175
    interfaces, 65
Treasury management system (TMS), 193,
    196, 197
Treasury operations, 62–63
    alternative financing sources, 188–89
    automation of financial reporting, 189–90
    best practices, 179–92
    case study on, 199–200
    centralized cash management structure,
        191–92
    consolidation of banking partners,
        186–87
    enabling technologies, 193–99
    float types, 177
    goals, 177
    implications of effectiveness, 175–79
    investment policies, 185–86
    monitor financial exposure, 190–91
    optimization of, 171–201

reducing cost of capital, 187–88
    responsibilities of, 63
Tyco, 22

U
UPS, 42–43
Upstream/downstream channel
    relationships, 6

V
Value, 48
    added, 79
Value-added network (VAN), 120
Value Chain, 6, 7
    defined, 46
Value-gap analysis, 41, 42
Velocity, 41, 82
    cycle times and, 84
Vendor-managed inventory (VMI), 157

W
Wal-Mart, 37–38, 154
Weighted average cost of capital (WACC),
    15, 106, 187
Win-win partnerships, 105–15
Workflow automation (WFA), 101
Working capital, 28, 135
    defined, 50–58
    formula for, 51
    general ledger accounts and, 53
    liquidity and, 50, 52
    negative, 29
    optimization of, 51, 184
    processes, 50
Working capital processes, 59–63
    accounts payable, 60
    accounts receivable, 59–60
    procurement, 61–62
    treasury operations, 62–63
Work in process, 80
    equation for, 80
Work-in-process inventory, 47
WorldCom, 22, 172
World economy, evolution of, 62

Y
Y2K scare, 38, 39

Z
Zero balancing, 195
Zero-sum game, 49
Ziglar, Zig, 34, 35